NOTES FOR GOATS
AND OTHER TATE BRITAIN PAINTINGS

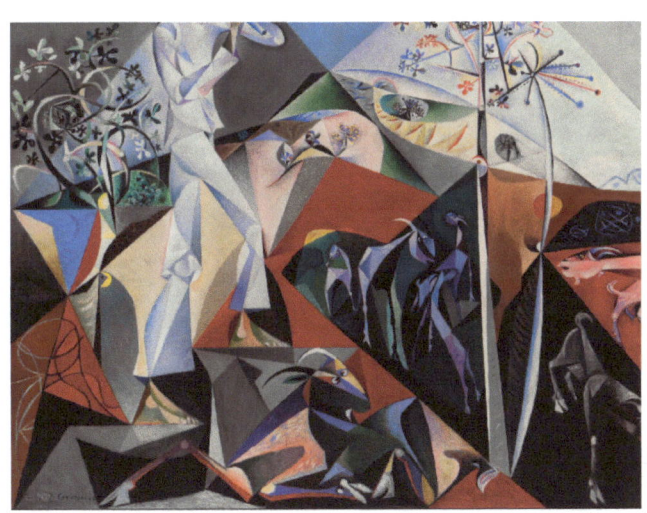

Susanne Carr

© Susanne Carr 2012

All rights reserved. No part of this work may be reproduced or stored in an information retrieval system without the permission of the publisher and relevant copyright holder.

First published in Great Britain by WritersPrintShop 2012

ISBN 978-1-78018-513-2

The right of Susanne Carr to be identified as the author of this work has been asserted by her in accordance with the Copyright, Designs and Patents Act 1988.

Copyright of images:
The pictures featured are all in Tate Britain, London. Their rights to the mechanical copyright of the images is acknowledged. They are all ©Tate, London 2012.

Acknowledgements:
Permission was granted by the following artists to reproduce their work and this is gratefully acknowledged:

Mr and Mrs Clark and Percy by David Hockney

Nataraja by Bridget Riley

Thanks are also due to the estate of Mr William Nicholson

The helpful approach of Amelia Morgan, and the staff at Tate Images, is also acknowledged.

To my sister Rachel, for all her help and encouragement

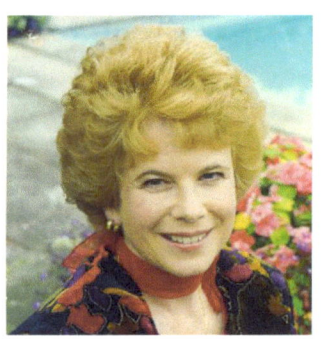 A vein of idiosyncratic originality runs through the history of English art, which at times could almost be called eccentricity. My choice of twenty English paintings in Tate Britain reflects this. I have not chosen mainstream artists such as Hogarth, Reynolds, Gainsborough, Constable and Turner. Instead my selection is from English painters, some of whom are less well-known, who reveal the freshness of personal vision and individuality, which is my theme. The works are not always on view, as Tate Britain can only show a fraction of its holdings at any one time; but these twenty paintings form my ideal one-room exhibition in the Gallery.

CONTENTS

1	**Bring on the Pearls!**: *Queen Elizabeth I*: Nicholas Hilliard	6
2	**Hare Heaven**: *Endymion Porter*: William Dobson	8
3	**Horses into Art**: *Mares and Foals by a River Landscape*: George Stubbs	10
4	**Sir Brooke by a Brook**: *Sir Brooke Boothby*: Joseph Wright of Derby	12
5	**Don't Make Me!**: *Elohim Creating Adam*: William Blake	14
6	**Under Palmer's Duvet**: *A Hilly Scene*: Samuel Palmer	16
7	**Desert Rush Hour**: *The Flight out of Egypt*: Richard Dadd	18
8	**Too Much Information**: *The Awakening Conscience*: William Holman Hunt	20
9	**A Brown Study**: *The Doctor*: Luke Fildes	22
10	**A Hold-Your-Breath Bowl**: *The Lowestoft Bowl*: Sir William Nicholson	24
11	**Cruel Carousel**: *Merry-Go-Round*: Mark Gertler	26
12	**Cookham Redeemed**: *Christ Carrying the Cross*: Sir Stanley Spencer	28
13	**Paint Box in the Corner**: *Self-Portrait*: Hilda Carline	30
14	**Toytown-by-Sea**: *Hold House Port Mear Square Port Mear Beach*: Alfred Wallis	32
15	**Battle of the Baddies**: *The Fall of Lucifer*: Cecil Collins	34
16	**Triptych of Terror**: *Figures at the base of the Crucifixion*: Francis Bacon	36
17	**Notes for Goats**: *Pastoral for PW*: John Craxton	38
18	**The Power of Paint**: *Lost Mine*: Peter Lanyon	40
19	**Interior with Shapes**: *Mr and Mrs Clark and Percy*: David Hockney	42
20	**Kaleidoscope**: *Nataraja* : Bridget Riley	44

1| Bring on the Pearls!

Queen Elizabeth I, c1575 - Nicholas Hilliard (1547-1619)   78.5x61cm

"Make an icon of me! Make me a goddess and the Virgin Mary!"

Thus I imagine the commission for this painting to the man whom the Queen had finally found to portray her as she wished: her limner, or miniaturist, Nicholas Hilliard. No wonder she snapped him up from the very first miniature he did of her, although this is a full size painting.

Exeter born, Hilliard had spent his youth in Geneva, where he must have seen Holbein's work, as he praised that master in his book on limning. One can see the influence of Holbein's intense scrutiny and attention to detail in this painting. Hilliard had entered the Queen's service at aged fifteen as an apprentice to her goldsmith.

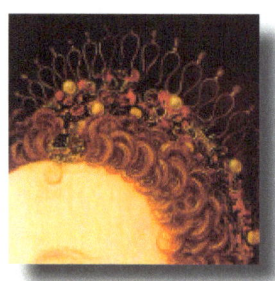

Elizabeth's image consultant Hilliard has done everything required of him. Nothing in the dark background detracts from her. The subdued tones of white, cream, pink and various browns quieten us. Her face is a flat white mask; she is a goddess Virgin Mary icon, untouchable and scarcely human. No lines or blemishes mar the airbrushed perfection of this old lady of about forty-two.

Her jewelled and impeccably curled hair (or wig) is topped by a gossamer halo headdress, and from it floats a diaphanous veil as translucent as silken wings. Her high lace ruff hides any possible crease of neck in cobweb strands of paint that were surely from a brush holding a single hair. The lace is repeated at her cuffs. Her refined hand delicately holds a Tudor rose, which is a flower also emblematic of that 'mystic rose' the Virgin Mary. The jewel at the centre of her neckline looks like another rose.

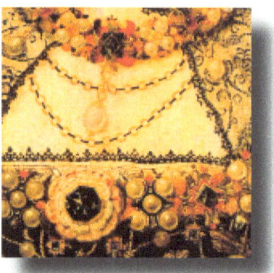

The large brooch immediately below it, in a soft pink that is echoed elsewhere in other adornments, is a phoenix. It rises from gold flames, renewing itself by fire, symbol of immortality and virginity. There is no need for any bedroom malarkey if you stay a virgin.

The Queen wears an intricately ornate garment that seethes and swarms with pearls, other jewels and gold embroidery. I do not know how she can bend her arm. Her white under-robe shows through her slashed sleeves like plump little pillows or luxury peanuts, encircling her upper body, white as her flesh and pearls.

At the bottom is a flurrying fandango of feathers: a muff, or a fan perhaps, for her other, hidden, hand.

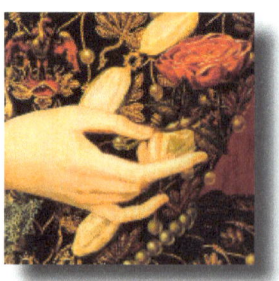

How many ladies damaged their sight making that lace, sewing on the pearls and embellishing the gown? Who is counting? No sacrifice is in vain for the Virgin Queen.

What could her servants and fellow monarch do but fall to their knees in awe?

Ticks all the boxes!

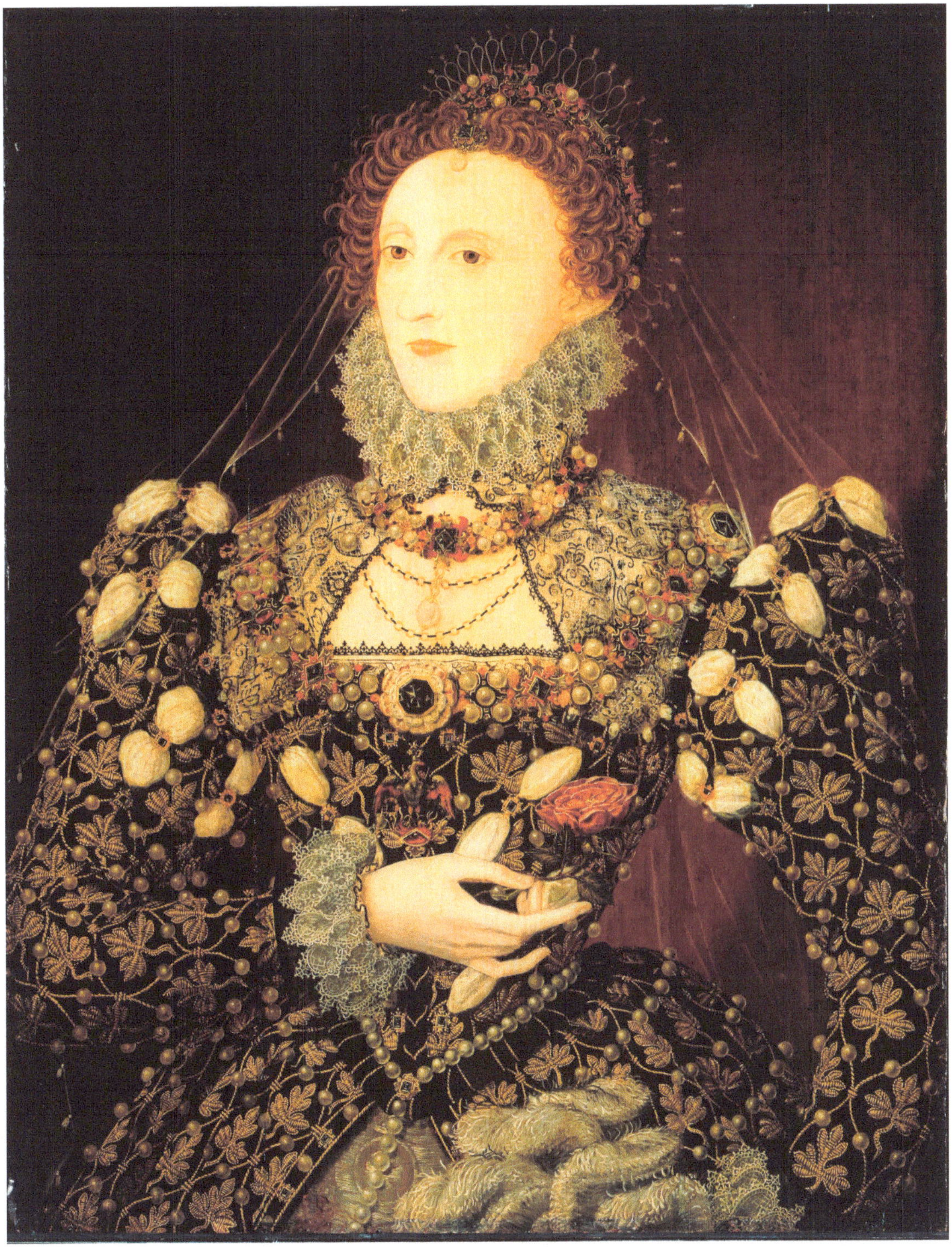

2 | Hare Heaven

Endymion Porter, c1643-45 - William Dobson (1611-46)   150x127cm

"Our little prince! He shall be called Endymion!" I imagine Mr Porter Senior saying at his son's birth, and then educating him for high office, learning Greek and the origin of his name.

Sure enough, Endymion Porter (1587-1649) became a man of culture and learning, devoted to literature and the arts. He was Charles I's trusted courtier as Groom of the Bedchamber, and one of the agents scouring Europe for paintings for the fabulous Royal Collection.

When the Court was in exile in Oxford during the Civil War, Charles I, for the first time, chose a native-born Englishman as his Court Painter, after the Germans and Flemings. His finest of these, Van Dyck, had died in 1641, and the following year he appointed his loyal servant William Dobson, who had followed him into exile.

Dobson was one of the first truly English painters, miniaturists apart. The little we know about him is that he lived an undisciplined life, dying at 36 soon after he came out of prison for debt. This is his outstandingly accomplished masterpiece.

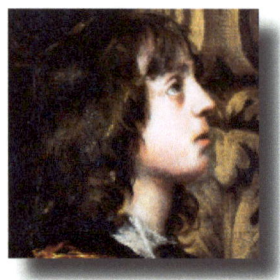

Both Dobson and Porter had doubtless examined Charles I's paintings, many of them Venetian, especially by Titian; and of course superb van Dycks. It was a resplendent source for a painter, when there was nowhere for an artist to train, and no other national painting collection to study.

Porter may have suggested this pose himself, which echoed a Titian Charles owned of the Roman Emperor Vespasian. The deep gold and browns remind one of Titian, but Porter's florid, unidealised face is quintessentially English.

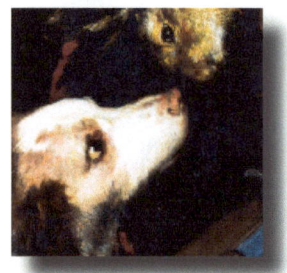

He is portrayed as a cultured connoisseur, which is emphasised top left by the bust of Apollo, Greek god of the arts. Bottom right, making a diagonal, is a classical low-relief sculpture of three figures representing painting, sculpture and poetry. The central figure of sculpture is carving Pallas Athene, Greek goddess of the sciences, arts and war. She holds a shield and spear, which could be significant as Charles I was at war when this was painted. We also see Porter as a sportsman and country squire. All that fabric of his voluminous hunting outfit must have encumbered his aim, as he has only managed to shoot a large rabbit or hare with his magnificent wheel-lock hunting gun. That gun makes a dramatic diagonal to counteract the one made by Apollo and the frieze.

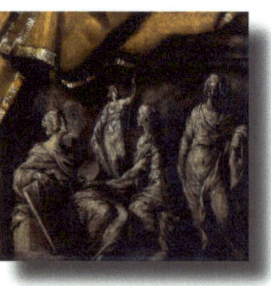

There is a small sub-plot on the left below the bust of Apollo, which upsets the composition a little. The page boy holding the dead hare looks up at Porter almost accusingly, as if about to cry. His eye is similar to that of the dog, its nose touching the hare's; dog's head and hare echoing the line of the gun.

This boy wears a touch of the only red in the painting: the colour of shed blood.

The gun points to the landscape beyond, where I can't help seeing the tree as a hare's nose, the tree trunk leading to his mouth, and the two cloud formations either side and above the tree as two big smudged eyes: a celestial hare in hare's heaven. Once seen, I cannot un-see it; and now I'm afraid it will be the same for you.

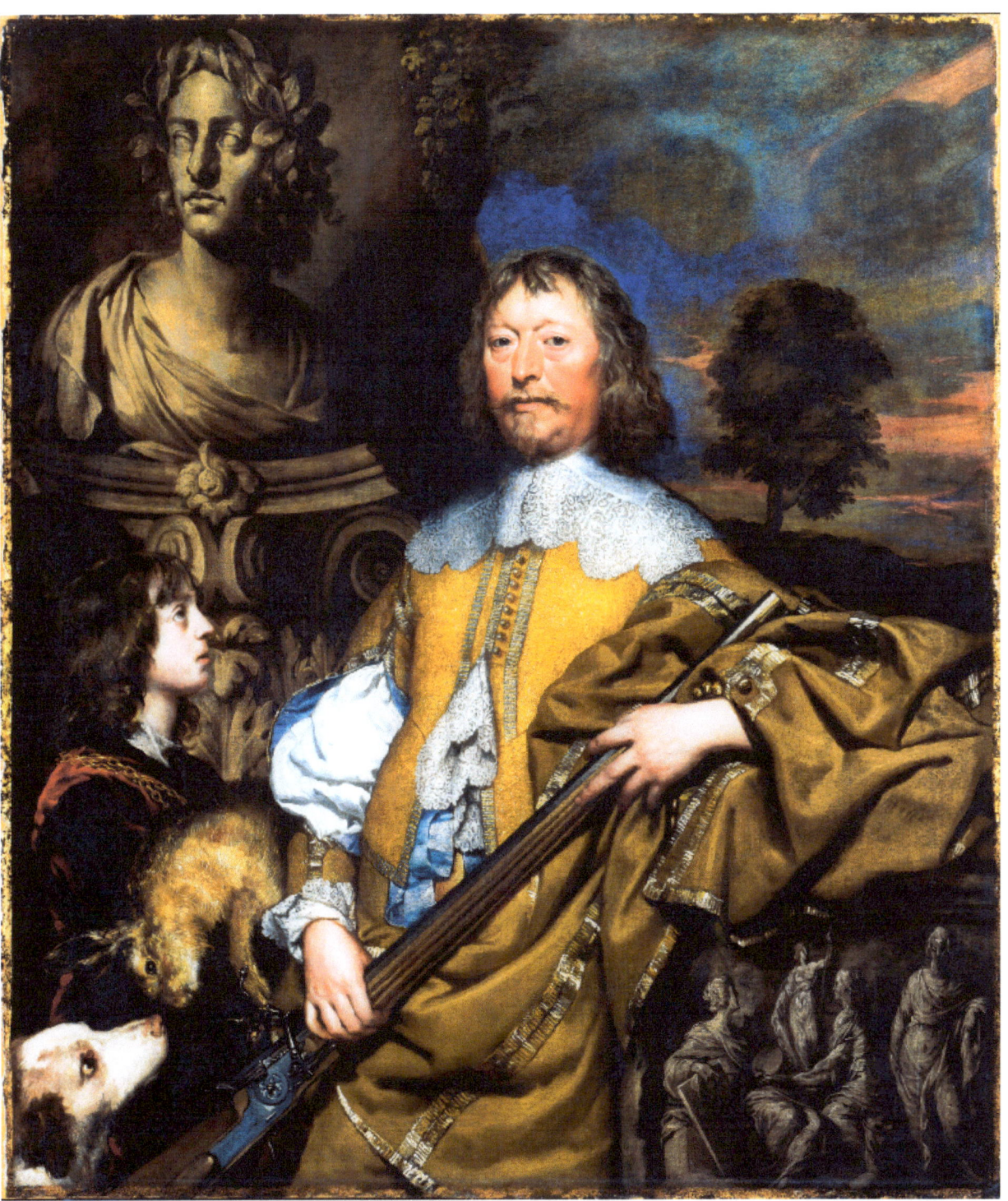

9

3| Horses into Art

Mares and Foals in a River Landscape, c1763-68 - George Stubbs (1724-1806)   69x102cm

This painting would be absolutely perfect without the landscape. Admittedly, the tree stretches out elegantly over the horses, its curves of trunk and foliage echoing the forms of the horses' necks and backs. The subdued tonal balance of the landscape is timeless and classical, its colours reflecting those of the horses, and the river leads the eye back in a peaceful spatial harmony. However, take it away and nothing, for me, would be lost.

The horses could then stand alone like a classical frieze, as they did on one of this series of about ten paintings of mares and foals that Stubbs did for his many aristocratic patrons in the 1760s. This one here, even with the landscape, I consider to be an eighteenth century masterpiece.

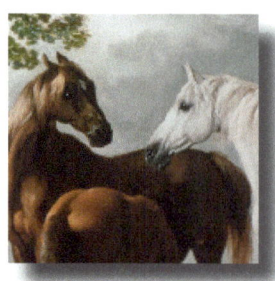

These are specific horses of one of Stubbs' noble patrons. His anatomical accuracy is absolute, which is all the more remarkable because he was the self-taught son of a Liverpool currier, drawing and dissecting from his teens. He studied human anatomy in hospitals and dissected other animals as well. His total knowledge of equine anatomy came from solitary years of arduous, smelly and dangerous toil dissecting them as they were suspended from a hoist he designed himself. He filled their veins with wax to preserve their shape, dissecting all their muscles and flaying them down to their skeletons. He drew all his dissections with the precision of a Leonardo, publishing and engraving several books, one of which, *The Anatomy of a Horse*, was published in 1766.

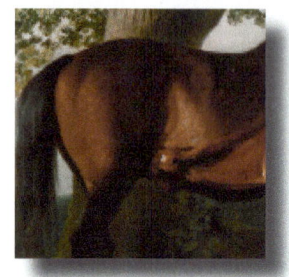

The composition is faultless, with a classical purity of design that Stubbs learned from studying after the antique in Rome, where a patron paid for him to go in 1754. There is a highly sophisticated sense of rhythm, interval and shape, each horse being placed with a refined sensibility.

The dark brown mare on the left turns towards the grey, which faces into the composition, the central mare poised between them. The feeding foals echo each other's poses, so that five horses have only three faces visible: a brilliant device that makes the placing of those three faces all the more flawless. The left profile is just clear of the central horse, making a magnetic sliver of space between them. The middle mare, whose back is overlapped by the grey's muzzle, turns gently to face her in a three-quarter profile. The grey's back leg, held at ease, is placed precisely, angled into the picture, thus uniting the composition as a whole. The oval that all the horses make together is sublimely designed.

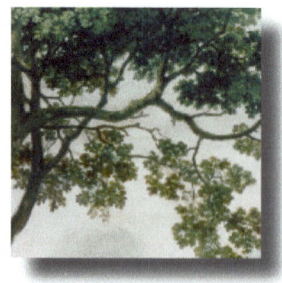

The shapes the pale sky makes between the horses are as exquisitely judged as the positioning of the horses themselves. Their curved backs, necks and rumps stand out against the sky in what I can only call a melodious way, like gentle waves.

In all these ways Stubbs has transcended his subject matter of five specific horses into the realms of art.

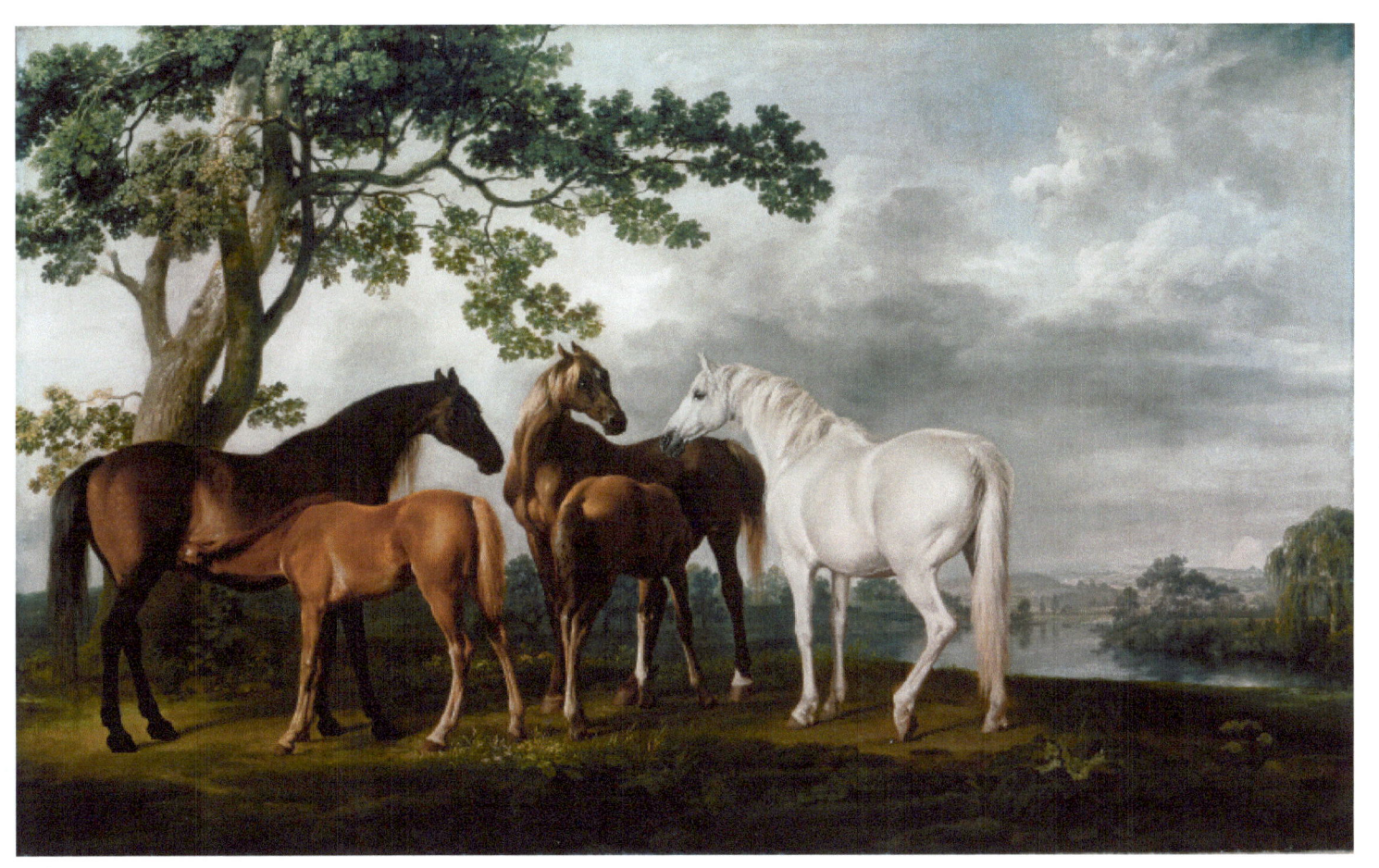
11

4| Sir Brooke by a Brook

Sir Brooke Boothby, 1781 - Joseph Wight of Derby (1734-97)   147.5x205.5cm

What on earth is this style icon doing lying down on the ground? It is the only eighteenth century English painting I know of a man adopting the pose of a naked reclining Renaissance Venus, but elegantly clothed. It always makes me smile. The sitter Sir Brooke Boothby probably posed on a sofa in Wright's studio, and looks somewhat unconvincing in the mud.

The painting is a wonderfully subtle medley of browns, with touches of ochre in the sky and cream and off-white in Boothby's stockings and shirt. What a triumph of the variation of one tone, with the sharp observation of shadow and light, even though there is a feeling that Boothby posed indoors. Surely his pink puffy-eyed face would have been tanned brown if he had really been an outdoors man.

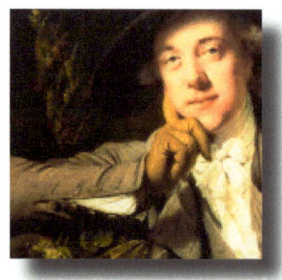

Sir Brooke Boothby was a nobleman in a line of baronets and a Derbyshire landowner, and was painted in 1781 by that most brilliantly original Joseph Wright of Derby. Both sitter and artist were keenly interested in the scientific discoveries and new ideas of the Industrial Revolution; and Wright painted some of these, such as his masterpiece *An Experiment with an Air Pump* in the National Gallery.

The somewhat effete-looking Boothby considered himself a philosopher and poet; and he and Erasmus Darwin, (grandfather of Charles,) founded the Lichfield Botanic Society, which may be why burdocks are sprawling over his stylish buckled shoes. He seems to be leaning on some extra-dirty further botanical specimens at the foot of a tree, his body making a languorous arc, from his rakishly-angled hat to his shoes in matching dark brown. His left arm is like one of the slender tree trunks and his right arm and book make two rhyming horizontals, echoing the angle of his legs.

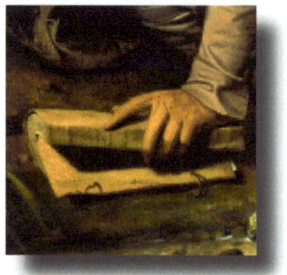

His kid-gloved hand is pointing to the author's name on the spine of his book: Rousseau, (Jean-Jacques,) whose manuscript of his *Dialogues* Rousseau entrusted to Boothby in Paris in 1776. Boothby translated and published it in England in 1780, two years after Rousseau's death. That famous philosopher and political and social theorist, Rousseau, influenced the Romantic Movement and the leaders of the French Revolution with his controversial novels and treatises. (Not to mention his theories of children's education, having abandoned all his offspring in a foundling home.)

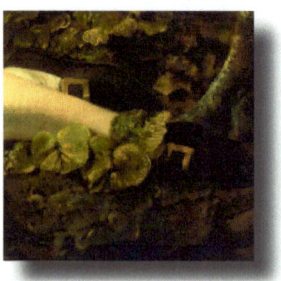

So Boothby is aligning himself with Rousseau's modern and unconventional ideas, trying to be a child of nature, as advocated by Rousseau, lying nonchalantly but unnaturally on the soggy banks of a brook, to pun with his name. His unbuttoned cuffs and waistcoat are making a style statement, showing how little he, a poetic intellectual, cares for social niceties of dress.

What an earnest young aristocrat he is, busily cultivating his sensibility in the age of the Enlightenment. I wonder, was it Boothby's idea to adopt that pose, or is Wright making fun of him without the affected nobleman realising it?

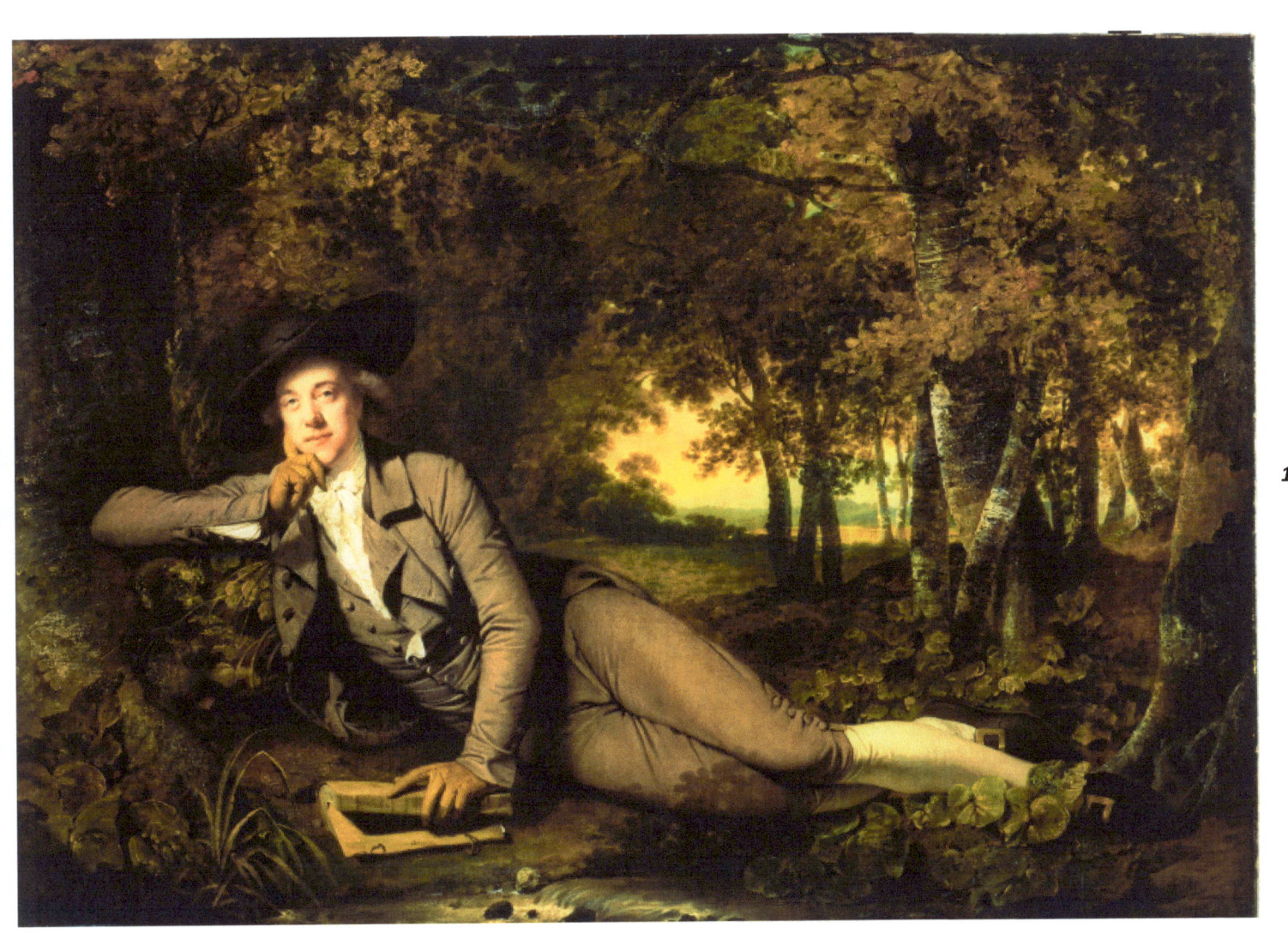

5| Don't Make Me!

Elohim Creating Adam, c1795/1805 - William Blake (1757-1827)   43x54cm

Poor old Blake. He often painted tortured figures bent over or howling in distress, like an eighteenth century Francis Bacon. He was a highly imaginative visionary and could see and hear his mental images and spirits of the dead. He claimed that he wrote and illustrated his epic poem *Millton* after that poet and other 'authors in eternity' appeared to him in his Lambeth home and dictated it to him. They took him to Felpham in Sussex, which he said was Paradise. He had conversations in Heaven and said: "A man who has never in his mind and thoughts travelled to Heaven is no artist". Wordsworth thought that Blake was mad; but, madman or not, Blake left an extraordinarily original body of poetry and visual art. Tate Britain has a very large amount of the latter.

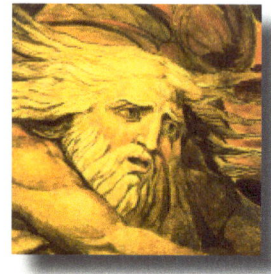

So what are we to make of this frightening Elohim – a Hebrew word for God – creating Adam as in Genesis 2:7? A heavy-winged God, looking as if he has been carved out of wood, swoops over Adam like an oppressive tyrant, dragging him out of the earth. With His left hand He gathers more earth to finish creating Adam, who seems as yet to have only one arm and leg; whilst possibly making Adam's head with His other hand. Adam opens his mouth to take his first breath, which looks like a woeful cry, as he flinches from being created. His arm is flung out in distress and a very large worm winds around him, either holding him down or being the matter out of which man is being created. Or it could be the tempter serpent already about its business?

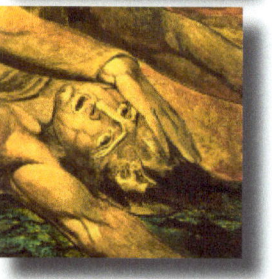

God is a cruel God. He is not looking at what He is doing, so He does not notice Adam's despair as he is being imprisoned in a material body, unable to float free as a spiritual being. That is how Paradise was lost for Blake: in the act of giving Man a body, not when he was expelled from Eden.

All of Adam and most of God is contained within a semicircle, as if earth and man are being created simultaneously. Dull blue and red bursts of light are radiating behind the semicircle/earth in the shape of a batwing, and all is formless void beyond. The compositional lines are mostly horizontal, which makes one feel as if Adam is being pinned down and his spirit is unable to get away from being incarcerated in a physical body.

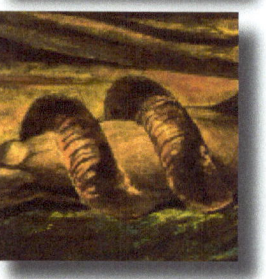

The colours are all appropriately earth colours, which also had the advantage of being the cheapest, and Blake was poor. The browns are rich and varied, with warm reddish tones that are beautifully modulated. The watercolour tints are skilfully applied and merged, for Blake despised oil painting. It is one of his many prints made in his characteristically novel way. He painted his picture on smooth millboard in thick colours, quickly before they dried. Next he placed paper on the image and took prints whilst the paint was wet, subsequently working over the resultant prints in pen, ink and watercolour.

So each print was an original, like Blake himself – a one-off mystic, idiosyncratic original.

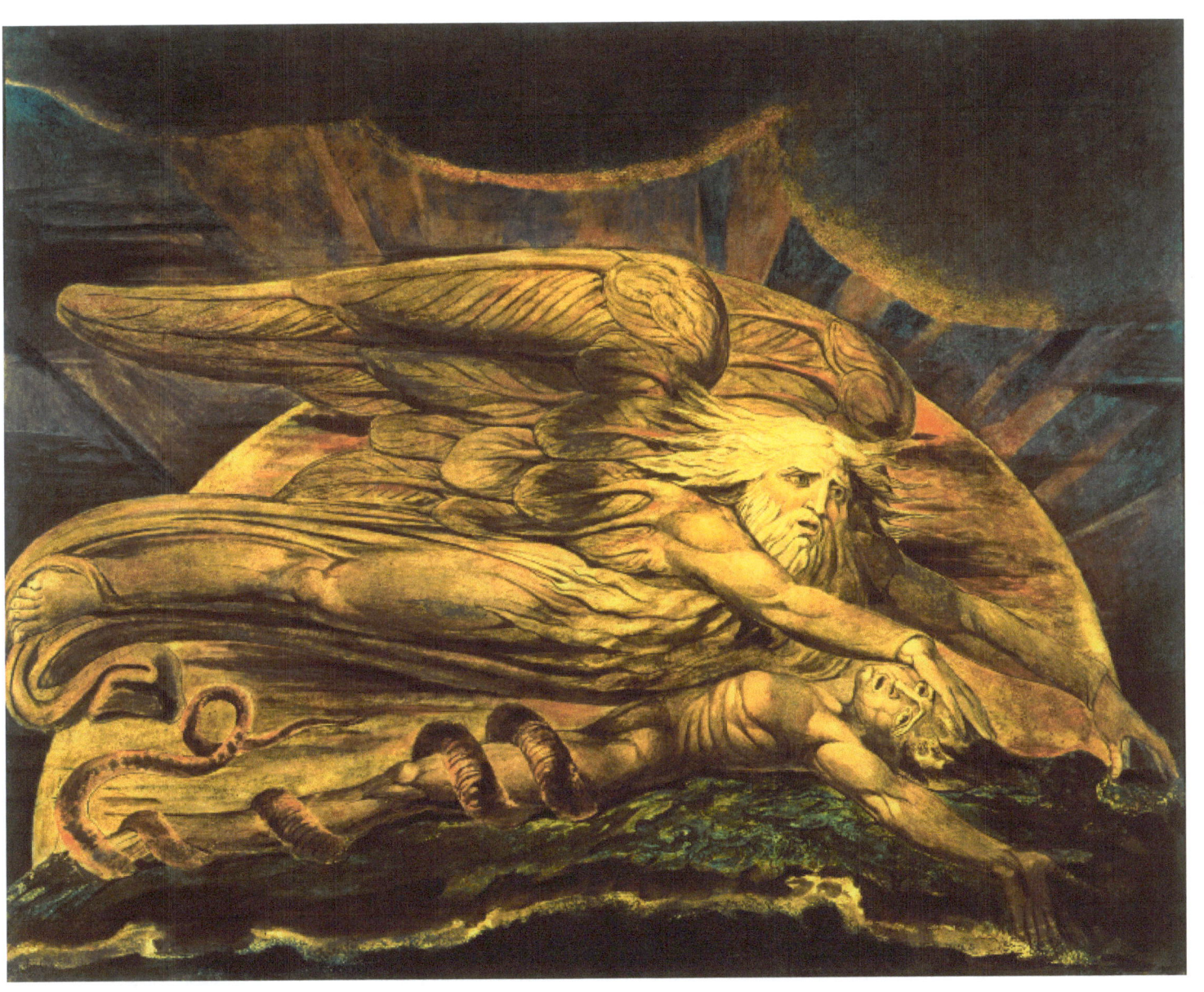

15

6| Under Palmer's Duvet

A Hilly Scene, c1826-28 - Samuel Palmer (1805-81) 20.5x12.5cm

Samuel Palmer had a paraffin lamp that he called Nancy. He sometimes dressed as a parson and liked to be called 'Reverend' as he tended the weeds in his garden. He is one of our quintessentially English eccentric artists, and it is difficult to believe that he is contemporary with the declamatory Delacroix.

Palmer's creative spirit leapt to life when he was introduced to Blake in 1824 at the age of 19 and Blake was 67, and he was forever entranced by the older man. Blake had made some wood engravings in 1821 illustrating Virgil's pastoral poems *Eclogues*, and Palmer was smitten by them with these often-quoted words: 'They are visions of little dells and nooks and corners of Paradise, models of the exquisitest pitch of intense poetry…a mystic and dreamy glimmer as penetrates and kindles the inmost soul.'

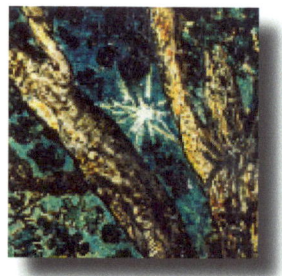

Palmer's 'inmost soul' and visionary powers were kindled in and by Shoreham near Sevenoaks in Kent, where he lived from 1826-33, before marriage and fatherhood intervened. His most spellbinding years were spent there in 'a village the devil had not yet found out' where he went on nocturnal ramblings. It was a mystic paradise for him in the same way that Cookham was to be for another English eccentric in the next century: Stanley Spencer.

Thus *'A Hilly Scene'* could illustrate a verse from one of his own 'epic poems,' as he called them:

> 'Low lies their home 'mongst many a hill
> In fruitful and deep-delved womb,
> A little village safe and still
> Where pain and vice full seldom come'

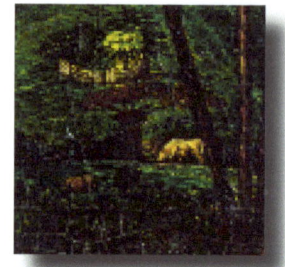

Here, all is 'safe and still' in a densely-worked tempera (pigment, water and egg-yolk) painting; no oil for Blake and Palmer. I imagine Palmer bent over the paper, holding his breath in concentration, as he worked over the dark thicket of tones, as he did with his etchings. It encapsulates his utopian dream of elysian fields, with roundly swelling hills like a tea cosy, below a star and harvest moon and glimpses of half hidden dwellings and a tiny animal grazing. The trees curve towards each other in a gothic arch, protecting the spiritual presence represented by the small country church. Nothing will harm us in this fruitful field.

A gate in the wicket fence is open to reveal tall ears of bursting wheat, ready to be made into the staff of life. No farmer would leave his gate open for his animals to start the harvest; but reality and toil do not feature in Palmer's work. Neither does correct perspective in the gate.

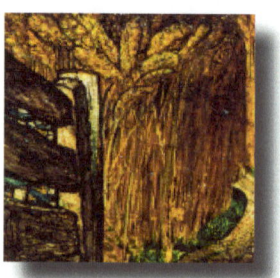

The best word to describe *A Hilly Scene* is the German word *gemütlich*, which means cosy, snug, agreeable, like being under a duvet. It is a scene that is comforting, eternal and forever safe.

It did not stay safe for Palmer, however. His three-year-old daughter died in 1847; and his adored son, the ambitiously named Thomas More, died aged 19 in 1861. Palmer's mysticism and rural vision were snatched away from him for ever.

But I hope that in later years, Palmer could pick up Nancy and look closely at his early work such as this one and find some shreds of comfort remembering that, in his youth, he had captured Paradise.

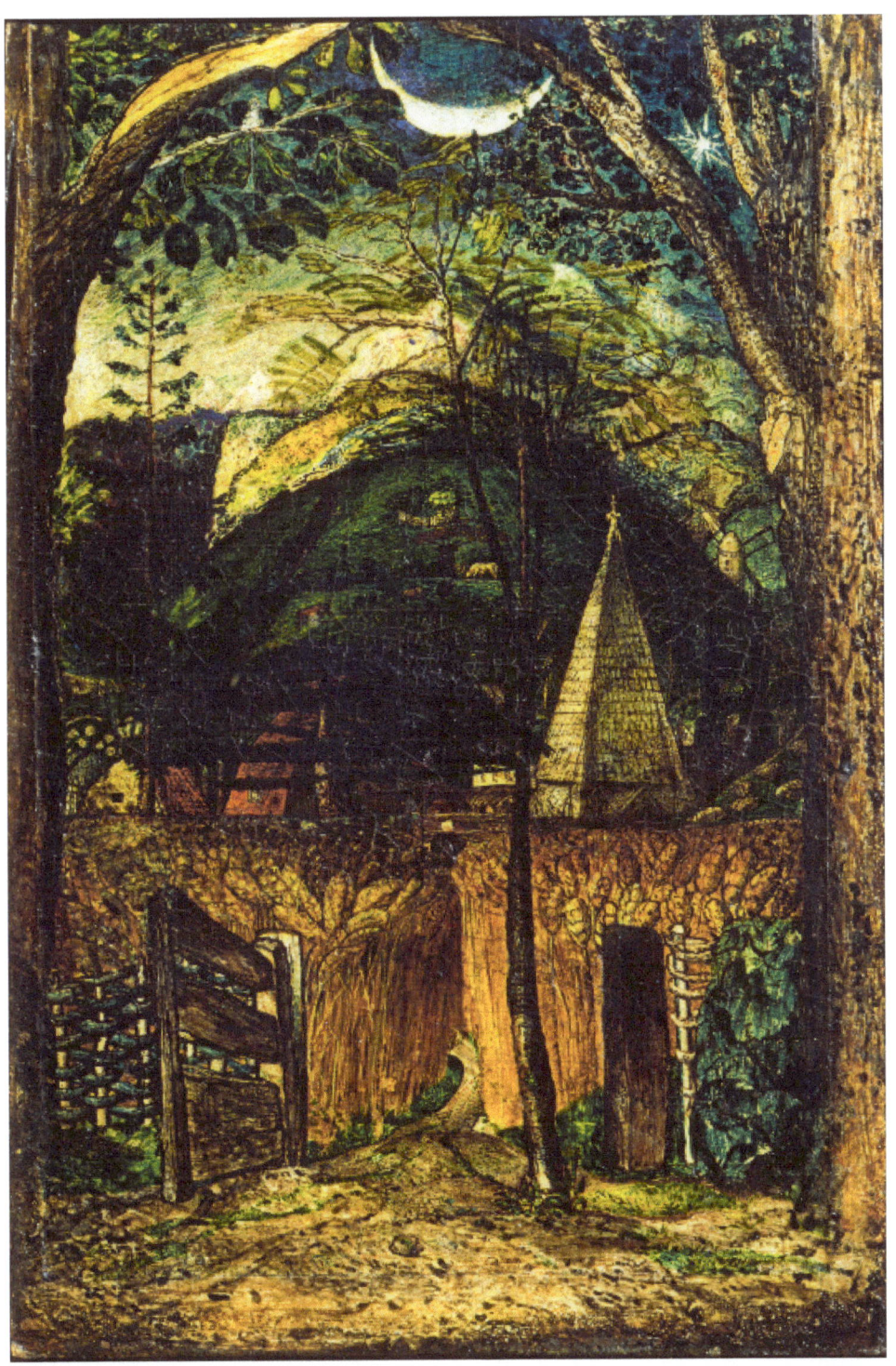

7| Desert Rush Hour

The Flight out of Egypt, 1849-50 - Richard Dadd (1817-89)   101x126.4cm

I am not sure what is going on here. It is as if Dadd has crammed all his sketchbook drawings into an incredibly complex picture, like the 'write all you know' exams in the old days. All is chaos and pandemonium, as myriads of people carry on multiple activities, right up to the ochre mountains in the background.

Perhaps it would help if we knew something of the artist. Dadd lost his mother when he was six, and his step-mother at 12. By then there were nine children to be raised alone by his father. Later, Dadd was a brilliant Royal Academy student, winning prizes and liked and feted by all.

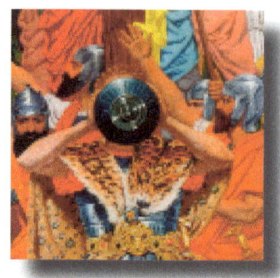

In 1842 he was invited to be part of a ten-month tour of Europe and the Middle East, and he sketched all the time. Towards the end of these travels, he began to be paranoic, believing that he was being persecuted by devils. Back home, his devoted father could not bear to have him put under restraint. Dadd made careful plans, and took his father on a walk saying he wanted to unburden himself of something. He stabbed his father to death, thinking he was the devil, and escaped to France, trying to kill again.

In 1844 he was sent to the State Criminal Asylum attached to Bethlem Hospital, ('Bedlam,') to begin 45 years of incarceration. He was transferred to the new Broadmoor in 1864, for the rest of his life. He was allowed to paint. This painting was done in 'Bedlam,' and indeed the seething scene is a sort of Bedlam itself, maybe reflecting a tormented mind.

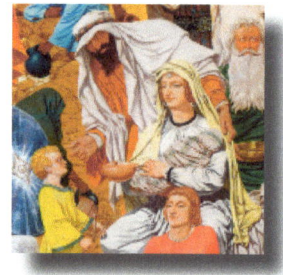

The title is not Dadd's. In the bottom right a seated woman holds a swaddled baby, with a man leaning kindly over her, looking vaguely like a Holy Family, in no great rush to leave Egypt. The woman is holding out a bowl to a boy in yellow, behind whom a goat wrestles with a grinning boy.

In the other corner, a boy in Prussian blue throws water from the foreground stream over a companion. The arc of water is arrested in flight, with hundreds of mesmerising scattered drops held still like an ornate diamond necklace. There are mounted horses and a camel to the left and dancers amongst the milling crowds to the right. Frenzy and clamour reign.

There seems to be no point in trying to make it all out, as one can with other paintings, because I do not think that there is any sense to be teased from it.

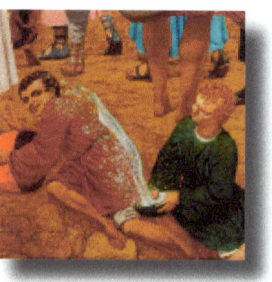

The whole spectrum of colours are here, with none predominating: all jumble together like a scattered jigsaw. I looked at this painting on the internet and quickly zoomed it in. Suddenly, all the pixels jumped into abstract coloured squares. It looked just like Bridget Riley's *Nataraja* (No. 20). The colours are all the same, except Riley has no black.

Her abstract parallelograms of colour make a greater impact on me than poor Dadd's incoherent muddle. I know he was ill, but his subject matter gets in the way of art appreciation. I don't have to try to work out what is going on with Riley. Dadd's painting is enormously skilful, but it wears me out.

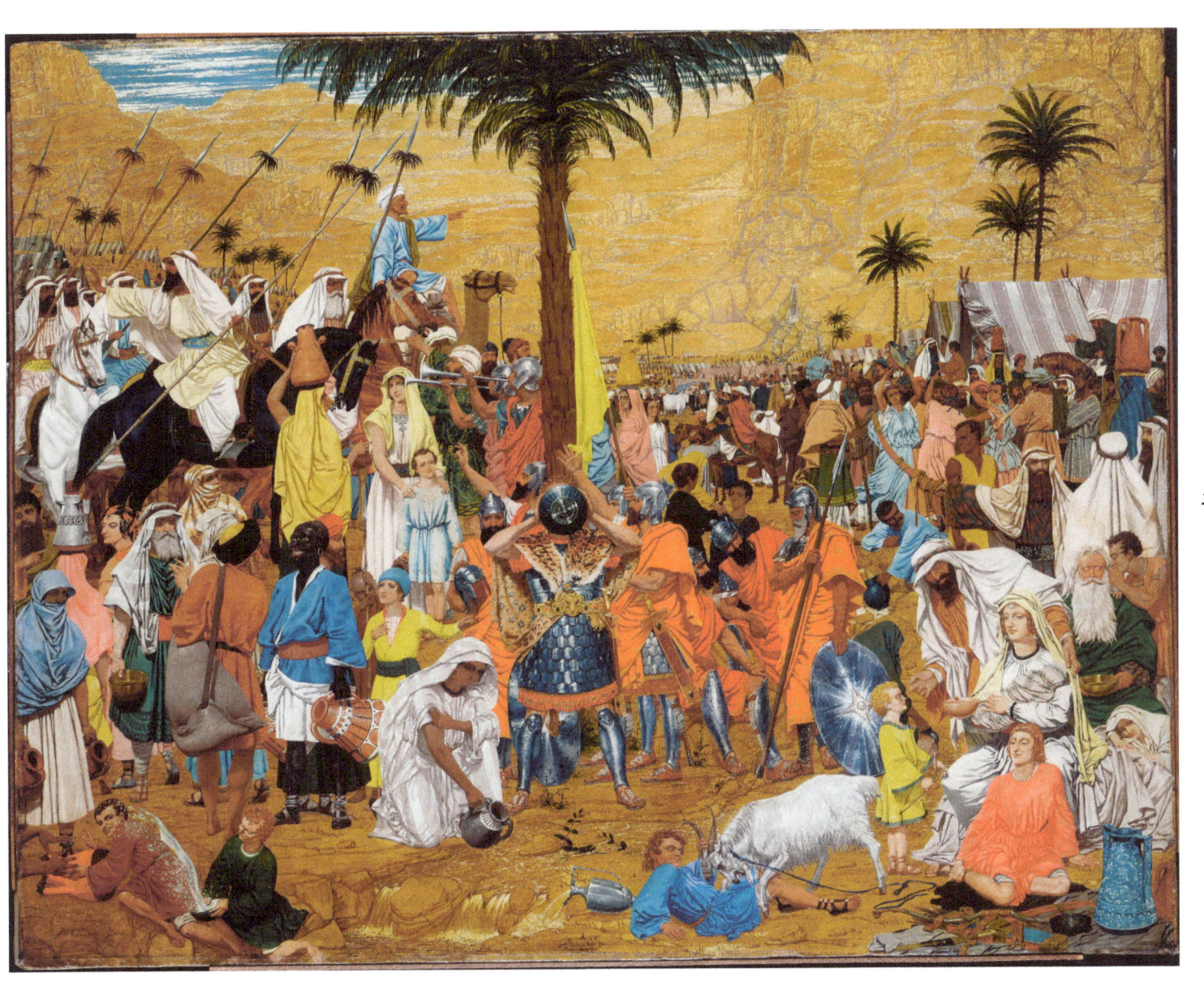

8| Too Much Information

The Awakening Conscience, 1853 - William Holman Hunt (1827-1910) 76.3x50.7cm

Holman Hunt was the very essence of a Pre-Raphaelite Brother. He believed that art should be the result of incessant toil, should serve Christ and have a moral. Further, it should be absolutely true to nature. Ruskin, who praised the Pre-Raphaelites, urged them to 'go to nature in all singleness of heart…rejecting nothing, selecting nothing and scorning nothing.'

The Pre-Raphaelite Brotherhood was formed in 1848, disapproving of art after Raphael, (1483-1520;) and in reaction against the state of contemporary art. There were seven members, three of them painters: Hunt, Rossetti, (1829-1919) and Millais (1829-96). Millais married Mrs Ruskin, but that's another story.

The Brotherhood's painting method was laborious and painstaking. They covered a canvas with white oil paint and varnish until it had dried as hard as ivory, drawing the design on that surface. Then they applied the colour bit by bit, over freshly-applied small daily patches of white oil paint, delicately stroking with sable brushes the colour on top of the skin that formed on each wet patch. The colours were brilliant and transparent, but a painting could take two years.

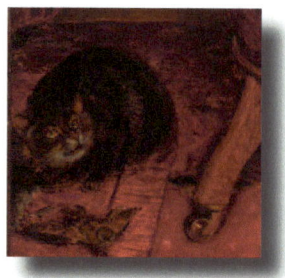

This impossibly infuriating method shows as you look inch by inch at this elaborate allegory. It is crammed full of detail, narrative and message. A man is with his mistress, and Hunt even hired a room in St John's Wood, where men went to be alone with their lady friends. (He should know, his mistress Annie Miller posed for the girl!)

The woman wears what would have been recognised as her underclothes, with rings on every left-hand finger except the third left. Her lover has been playing 'Oft in the Stilly Night' as can be read on the score, on what Ruskin called the 'fatally new' rosewood upright piano, not a grand piano with an antique patina. The song, not the best choice, is about a woman remembering her innocent childhood, hearing the 'still small voice of God', making the woman here start up in sorrow and remorse, her conscience awakened. Her face is not as agonised as it was originally, as the picture's first owner could not live with her distress and asked Hunt to tone it down.

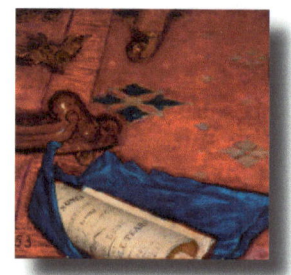

She is reflected stunningly in the mirror behind her, next to the wallpaper where vine and wheat grow untended. The scrolled song sheet in the foreground, still in its wrapping paper, reads 'Still Silent Tears.' Under the table, a cat toys with a bird, just as the man is toying with the girl. A dirty glove lies on the floor, discarded as the woman will be, without its mate. The tapestry on the extreme right is unravelling, its wools lie tangled on the bright modern carpet. The picture top right features the biblical woman taken in adultery…

As if this is not enough, Hunt designed the frame, with an admonishment from Ecclesiastes, decorating it with marigolds for sorrow and bells of warning.

Hunt's technical virtuosity is astounding. The composition is strong, the colours luminous, the detail extraordinary. It is just that there is too much detail, too many messages, too much information. It is very clever and I admire it, but it makes me want to go and lie down in a darkened room.

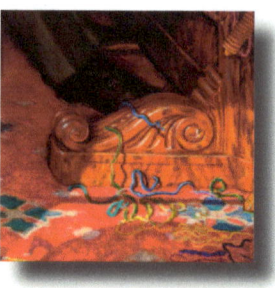

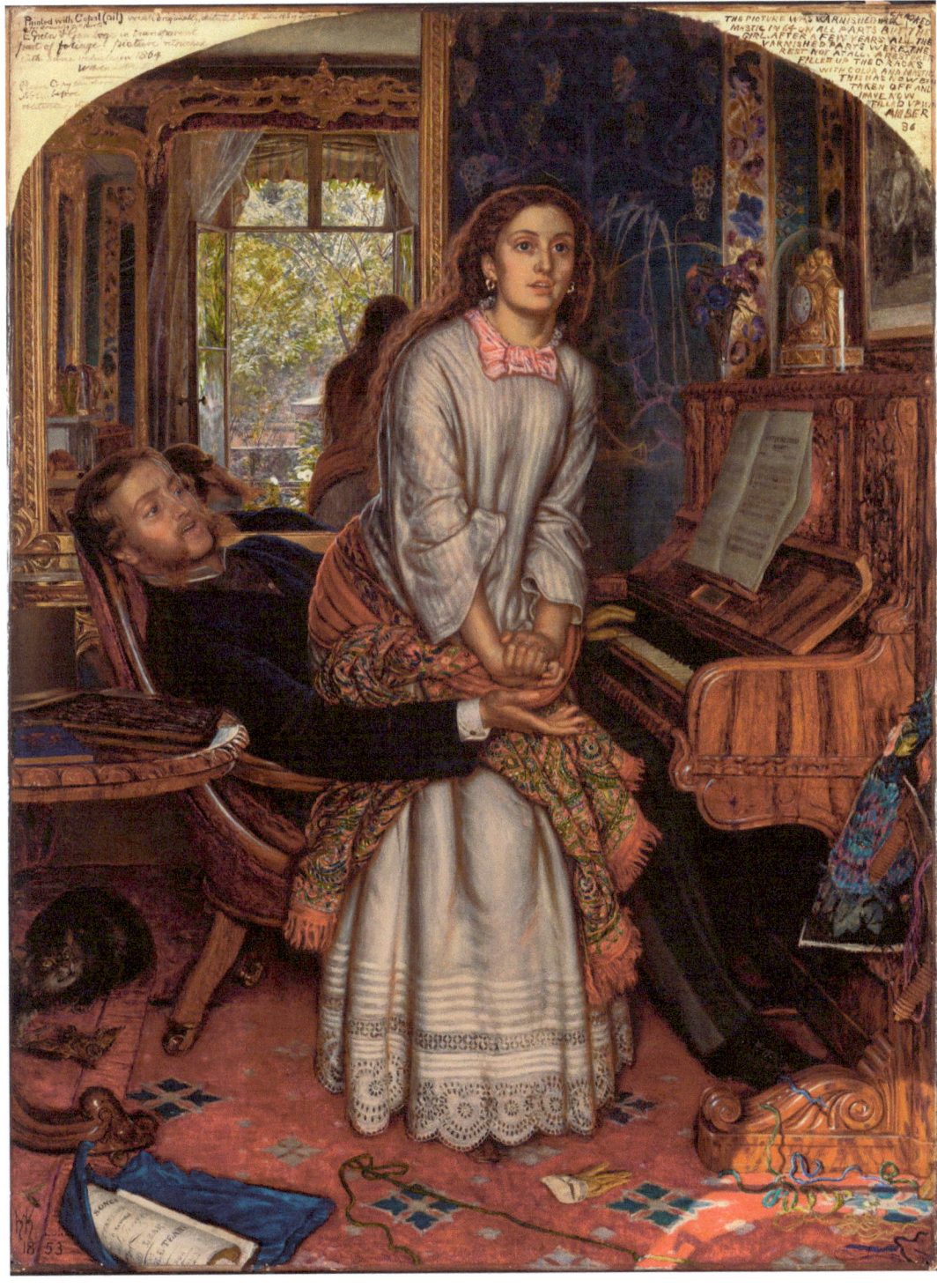

9| A Brown Study

The Doctor, 1891 - Luke Fildes (1844-1927) 73x148cm

This important painting for Tate Britain was commissioned by Sir Henry Tate, who gave his collection to the nation. The Tate Gallery was opened in 1897, six years after this poignant picture was painted. It was vastly popular at the Royal Academy in 1891. Agnew's print of it was a phenomenal success, and it featured on two postage stamps. Since Tate made his fortune from refining sugar, we can indulge in a sticky wallow.

Fildes chose the subject for this commission, a theme that could not be further from that of his contemporary Monet (1840-1926.)

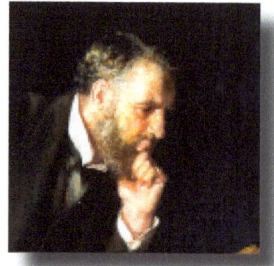

We see a devoted family doctor leaning forward, chin in hand, anxiously watching his small patient through the night. It is obviously a poor cottage, for the child's makeshift bed is two unmatching chairs, with a mattress of what looks like raggedy pelts and possibly another animal skin is a blanket. We know that the doctor will not charge his fee.

A lampshade to the left is angled to illumine the child. Medicine in bottle and cup has been administered, as has simple food on the right. Life is as fragile as the feathers on the floor.

Fildes is a master of composition. Two diagonals in an inverted V meet at the doctor's foot, so that we enter and share the tense vigil. A tight parallelogram is made by the doctor's back, the diagonal from his head to the child's flushed face in the lower centre of the painting, the angle of the patient's pathetically thrown-out arm, the infant hand to the doctor's left hand. This makes a concentration on the scene and increases the tension more than if, for example, the doctor was leaning back and the pillow was seen straight on.

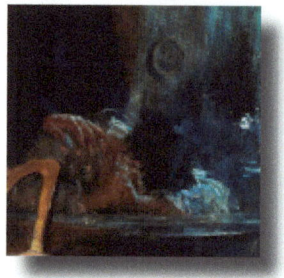

In the shadowy background, the standing father can be discerned, watching in an agony of suspense. Nearly lost in the murky gloom is the mother, her upper body collapsed over a table, her head in her anguished hands. She dare not look.

Dawn is just beginning to filter through the cottage window, indicating that the child has lived through the night's crisis, and all might yet be well. The two light sources of lamp and nascent dawn are acutely observed. The use of chiaroscuro (light and dark) is skilfully rendered both technically and symbolically. It suggests the darkness of night and despair and the tender glimmer of dawn and hope.

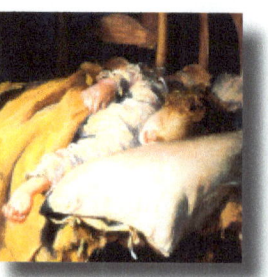

No bright colours distract our eye; only a wide variety of tones from cream, different shades of ochre and brown, to the darkest brown in the background. These sombre colours affect our feelings and draw us deeply into apprehension.

Fildes made a full-size cottage room in his studio, based on his own sketches. He superimposed his own window and the cottage window, so that the first pale light of dawn could be accurately depicted. Nothing was left to chance.

The Doctor may seem mawkish for today's audience, but, sadly, the death of a child was a reality for far too many families in 1891. What saves it even further from sentimentality is that Fildes painted it as a tribute to his own family doctor, who had cared so assiduously for his son Paul.

Paul Fildes died on Christmas morning in 1877.

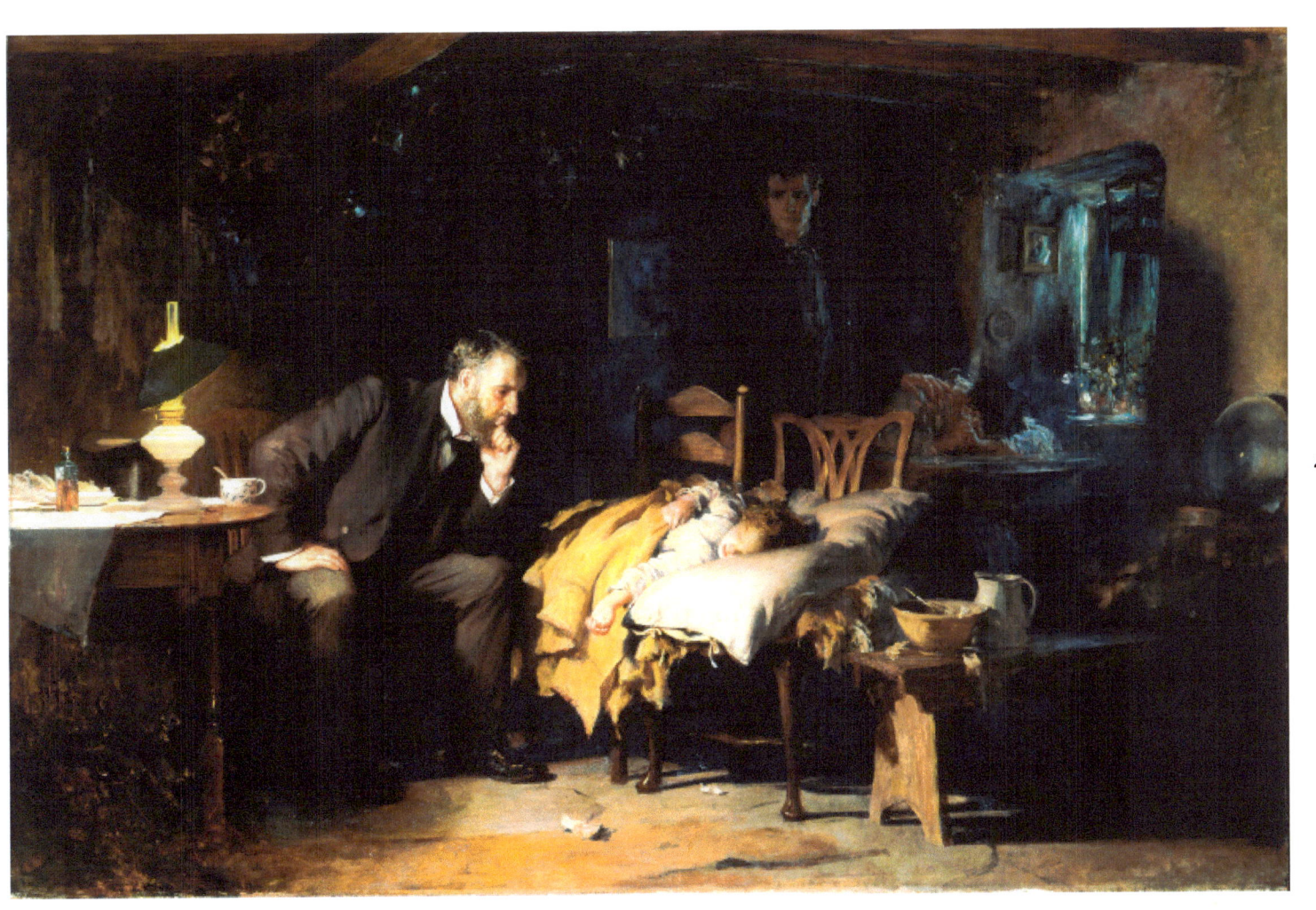
23

10| A Hold-Your-Breath Bowl

The Lowestoft Bowl, 1911 - Sir William Nicholson (1872 - 1949) 47.6x61cm

I find it difficult to explain why my response to this painting is so profound. It has very little in it: perhaps that is why I find it so alluring. It has one of the essential ingredients of what I think all great art needs: simplicity.

Sir William Nicholson was better known as a brilliant graphic designer, but here he is teetering on the edge of an abstraction that his son Ben (1894-1982) adopted entirely, as can be seen in Ben's *'White Relief'* also in Tate Britain.

Because there is no narrative, one looks at it very intently and almost forgets to breathe.

One sees juxtaposition, tone, shape and composition. The background is a very dark black/green/ brown. The platter or possibly lacquered tray is another slightly lighter deep brown, with other browns within it. The merest thread of cream on the edge of the tray right in the foreground is essential to the composition: cover it up and something is lost. Other striations of a lighter brown follow the curve of the tray's ellipse.

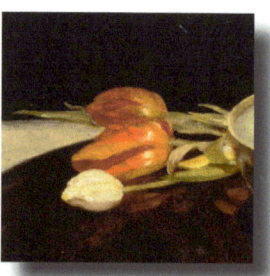

The bowl is a collector's item. Lowestoft porcelain was made from 1766 to 1802, so this piece is at the very least 109 years old. (However, now, since 2001 the porcelain is being made again.) Nicholson has painted his Lowestoft bowl to make it look as if it has a silver or gold lustre, but is probably a glaze. There are understated suggestions of reflections in it, and its interior is opaque greeny-cream as if it contains leek and potato soup, with the merest touch of a lighter spot in it. The bowl has a delicate pale gold rim inside, exquisite against the interior tone. The surface on which the bowl stands is the same shade as inside the bowl, subtly darker, like the tray, on the left hand side.

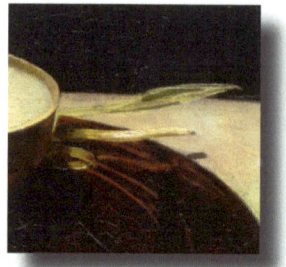

Three closed tulips, echoing the ellipses, pretend to be casually strewn behind the bowl, two of them a shiny orange with a deeper tone inside them. The other, smaller one in front is the same thick shade as the inside of the bowl. In fact, the tulips are placed with reverential exactitude, as are their stalks and leaves that extend beyond the bowl, each one a different length. Right in the foreground, again placed asymmetrically but at a diagonal to the bowl, is the lynchpin of the whole composition: a cream petal cast by the pale tulip, making a laconic half ellipse. Blot it out with your thumb and the whole delicate balance of the painting is lost. The petal is reflected, smaller, in the bowl. There are two lots of three: tray, bowl, petal, and three tulips. I want to look at it for a long time, and I am still forgetting to breathe.

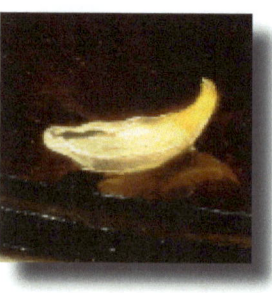

The Lowestoft Bowl appears to be simply a bowl on a tray with some tulips. But look at the echoing ellipses, the judicious placing of objects, the subtle tonal range and asymmetry. It is in fact highly sophisticated and of the utmost refinement. Not a brush mark could be changed without the whole composition falling apart. It has classical purity and perfection.

As I tear myself away from it, I take a deep peaceful breath.

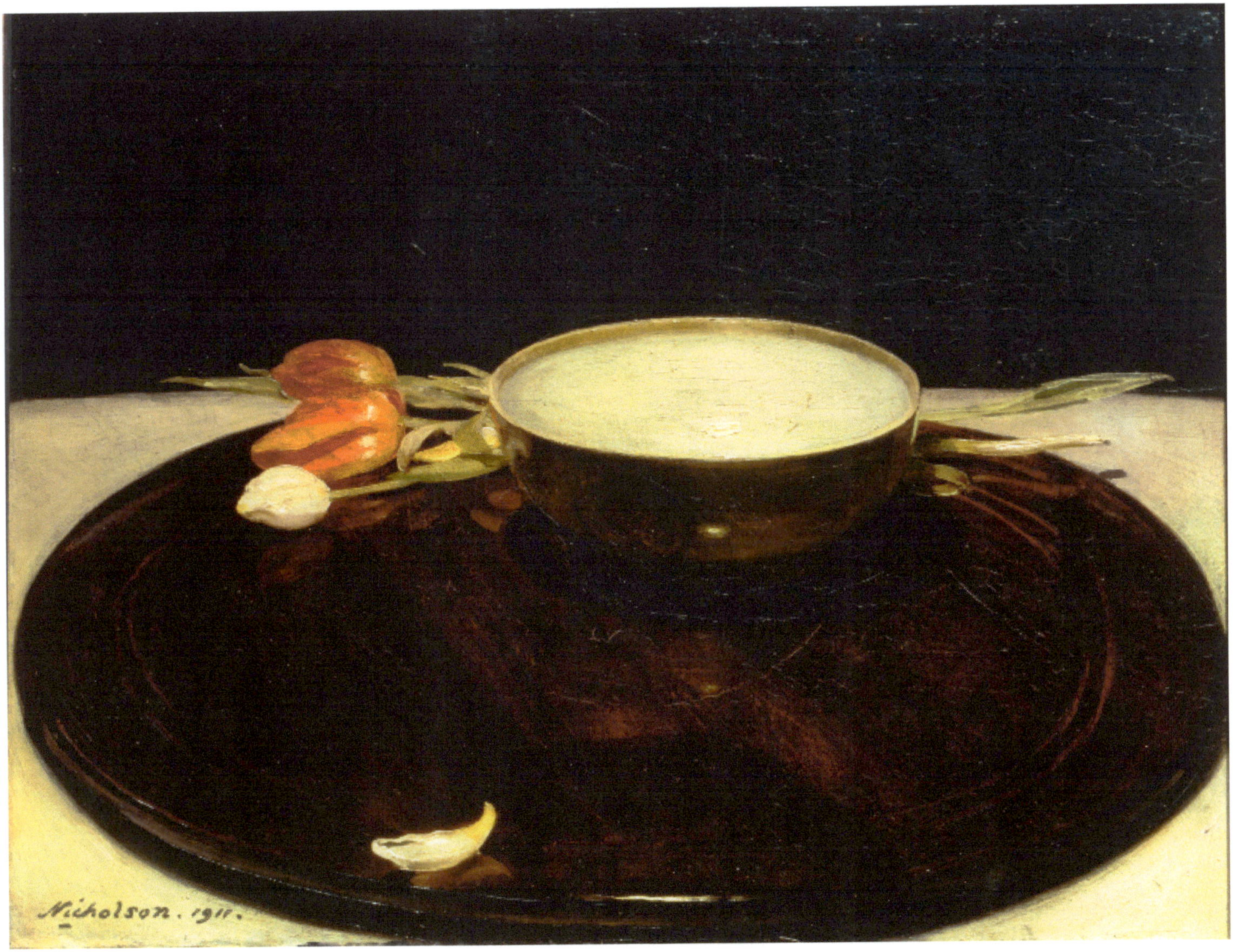

11| Cruel Carousel

Merry-Go-Round, 1916 - Mark Gertler (1896-1939)   189.2x142.2cm

This is more of a misery-go-round than a merry-go-round. Nobody is having any fun, and the cries coming out of all the open mouths do not appear to be shouts of delight, but howls of horror.

The carousel is going too fast and the riders cannot get off. Speed is indicated by the icy blue-white horns at the top. The fairground horses' legs also look like multi-exposure photographs of movement.

There are no children on the horses. All the pigeon-breasted riders are adults, and they are in uniform, two with their ranks on their upper arms. It is 1916 and WW1 is at its height. This merry-go-round is a demonic metaphor for the relentless round of wartime service and slaughter. The vertical orange rods are vital to the design, suggesting regimentation and an inflexible military machine.

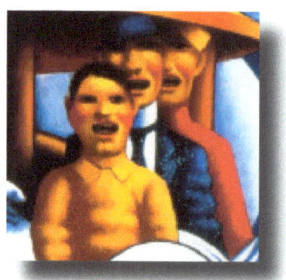

Gertler was twenty when he painted this, and he did not want to join the unspeakable and unpaintable abattoir. He was a conscientious objector. He has conjured this powerful image of war to express his anguish at it. A fairground ride of fun and relaxation has become a whirling vortex of fear. Somehow it is even more chilling than a depiction of mutual killing.

Gertler, who trained in London's Slade Art School, has harnessed his knowledge of colours to his own ends. Just as a roundabout should be fun, so should orange and yellow be happy and positive. Further, the main colours of orange and blue are complementary, opposite each other on the colour wheel. When they are placed next to each other, each colour seems more intense. However, Gertler has subverted the ostensibly joyous potential of orange, yellow and blue into something that jars violently.

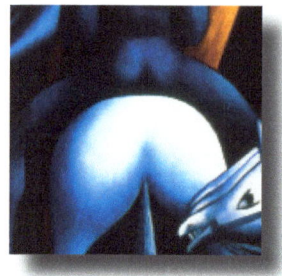

He also uses a black void; and white that modulates the crescent forms in the sky and the horses' rumps and necks, which make similar shapes. Gertler was good at design and rhyming shapes. The sailor on the left with his back to us has a small blue bottom that is the same, but smaller, as the rear of the horse on which he sits. It is the only part that makes me smile.

He has also hijacked conventional one-point perspective, (where parallel lines appear to converge on the horizon;) to jolt the viewer and give a feeling of dislocation. A painting should have only one viewpoint. However, the carousel, the round world at war, is seen in tipped-up perspective, implying, perhaps, that all the riders will be flung to their deaths by centrifugal force. We are high up, looking down. Yet we look up at the triangular top of the ride: we can see its elliptical far side. The servicemen and horses are seen from yet another viewpoint, straight on. Gertler has distorted the rules so that we do not know where we are.

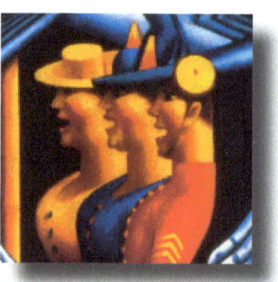

Fun has become fear, what should be children are uniformed adults, people and horses are machines, colour contrasts jolt, perspective is inconsistent. The round carousel-world is whirling towards self-destruction.

So was Gertler. In June 1939 he could hear the merry-go-round of war getting ready to start up again. He was Jewish. He chose his time to leave.

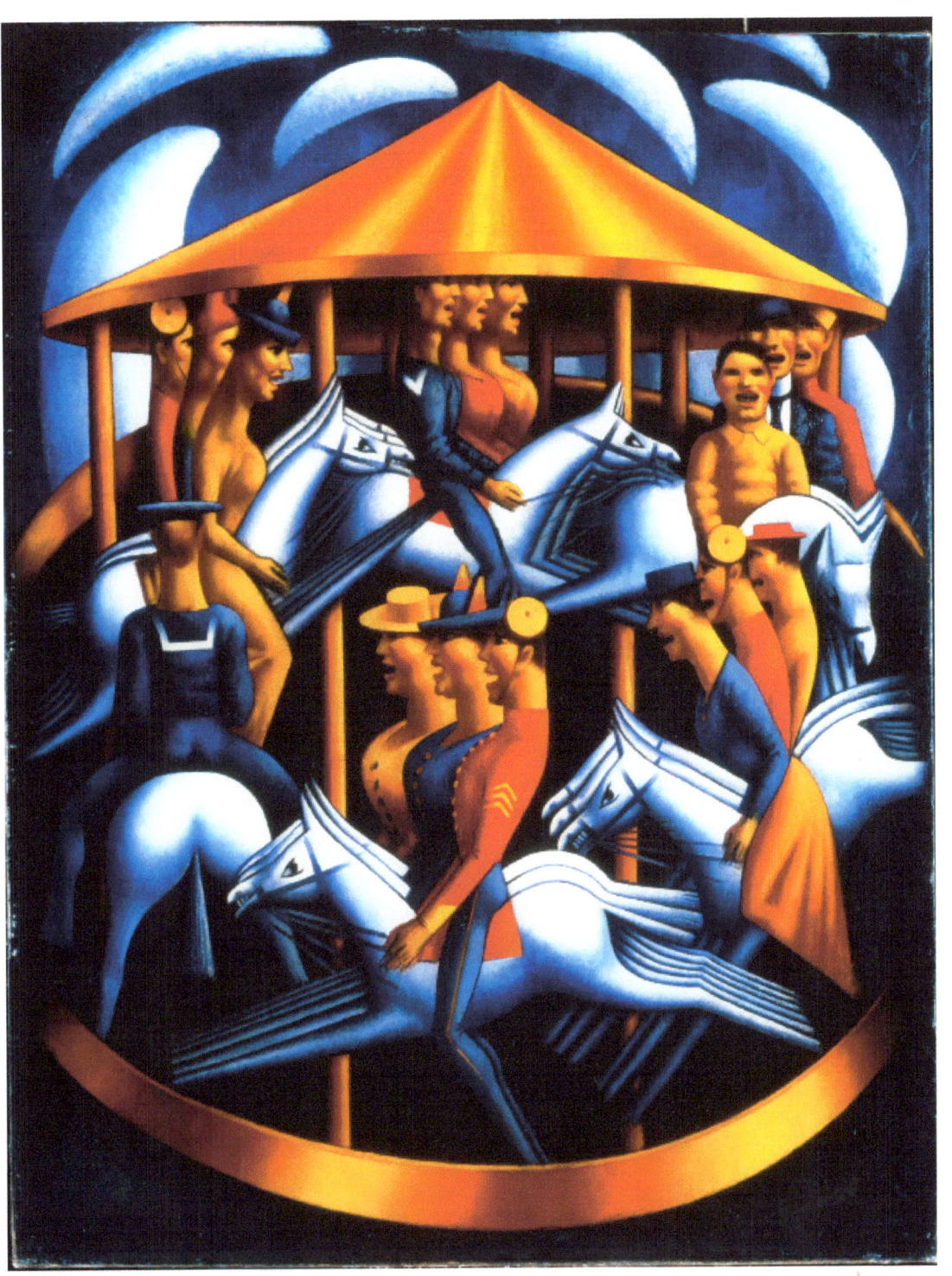

12| Cookham Redeemed

Christ Carrying the Cross, 1920 - Sir Stanley Spencer (1891-1959)   153x143cm

I imagine that one day Spencer leaned out of a window in 'Fernlea' in Cookham High Street, where the nine Spencer children grew up, and saw workmen carrying their ladders in the accidental shape of a St Andrew's cross; and he immediately transposed that into Christ on the road to calvary. So the painting could be one of his spiritual allegories or transmutations.

Spencer's soul was wedded to every brick and leaf in Cookham; he was even called 'Cookham' at the Slade. It was heaven on earth for him, as Felpham was to Blake and Shoreham to Palmer. He was a highly complex, multi-faceted, obsessional and imaginative man, who said that the aim of his art was redemption.

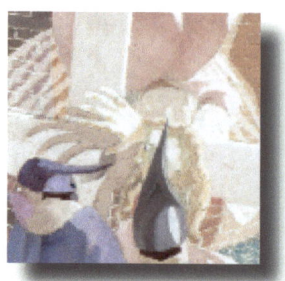

The road here is Cookham High Street, which was for Spencer a great big church, and his paintings were decorations for it, like the Stations of the Cross. That is perhaps why his oil colours are pale, like a fresco, as if it is one wall of his imagined church.

So Jesus carries His cross past 'Fernlea', next to the ivy-covered house 'The Nest'. His bearded near-invisible face, that of the Spencer father William, is in profile behind the third of the accompanying soldiers in pixie helmets. One can see Jesus's big white hand and its shadow at the top of the cross, getting ready for the nails. The builders are going about their tasks with their ladders, or maybe they will nail Jesus to the cross, and Jesus is getting on with redeeming mankind. The two crosses predominate and the other forms radiate from them. Three men shade their eyes as the Light of the World goes past.

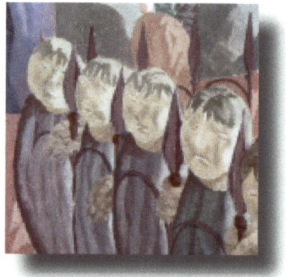

Seventeen people lean far out of every window of 'Fernlea' and one window next door. The flimsy curtains fan out on either side of them like angels' wings, so they could also be angels looking down from heaven. Spencer liked repeating shapes.

The bent female figure in the foreground could be both a grieving Mary and a distraught mother Annie Spencer, with her five sons lined up behind a barrier of railings, the tops of which they grasp like spears. They are ready to go off to war and sacrifice, like Jesus behind them. One son, Sydney, had indeed been killed, and Stanley had served in Macedonia in 1916.

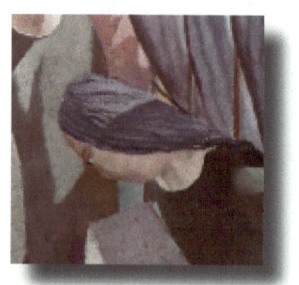

The pastel shades are united in soft pinks and greys, with a grassy patch below the cross looking like a cabbage leaf. In the top right, a cowl stands out against a threatening sky, that of Cookham's malthouse, which had been built by paternal grandfather Julius. Spencer has moved it from its actual position, perhaps to symbolise that man's presence.

One can see Spencer's love of painstaking detail in the pointing of the bricks on the left, and the ivy, which are painted more minutely than the moderately undefined forms of the milling crowd, almost as if blurred in movement.

Spencer's highest genius can be seen in his 1926-34 Sandham Memorial Chapel in Burghclere near Newbury and his WWII 'Shipbuilding on the Clyde' panels in the Imperial War Museum.

But here in Cookham, Jesus and he go about their business of redeeming mankind, one by death and one by art.

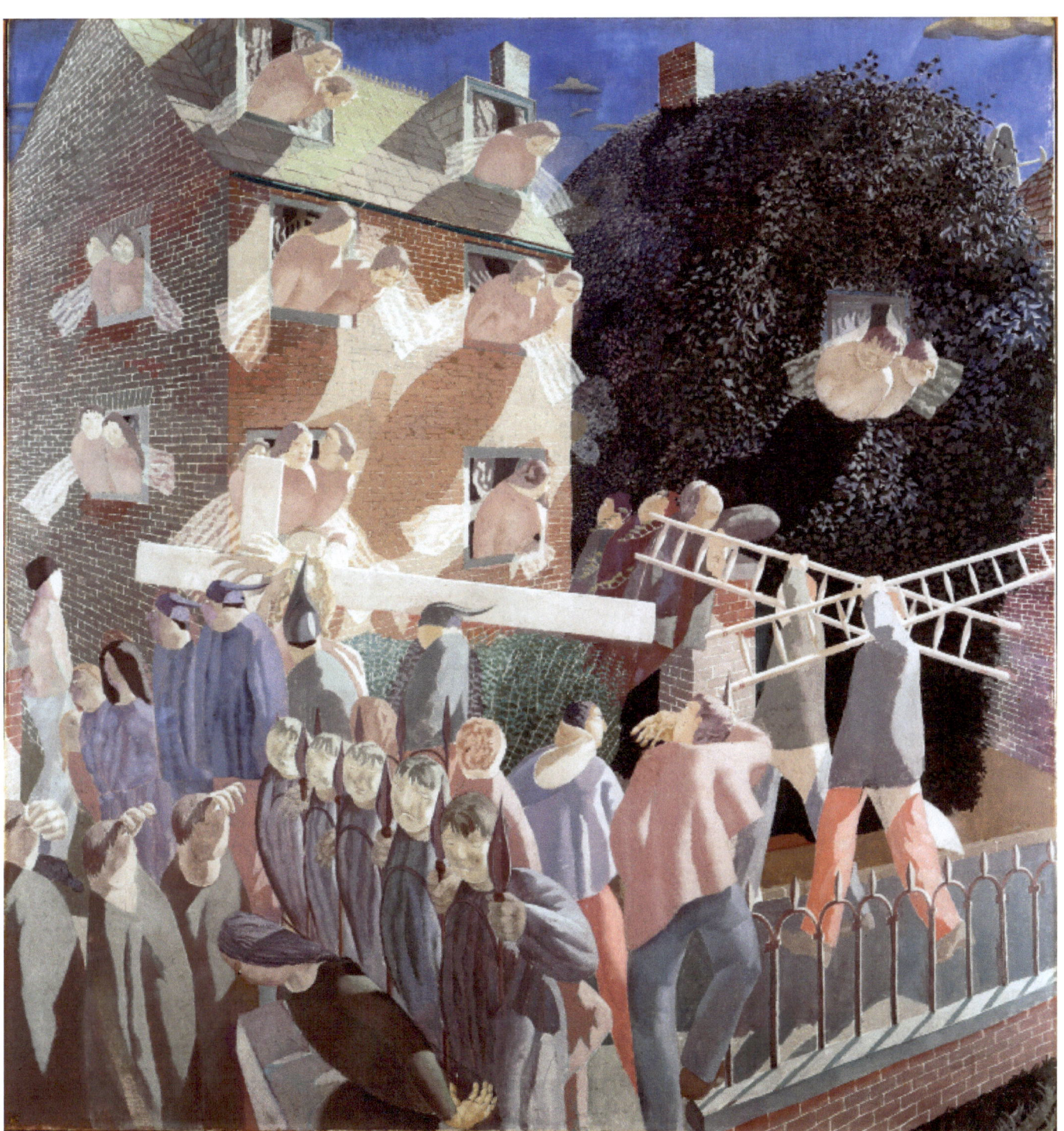

13| Paint Box in the Corner

Self Portrait, 1923 - Hilda Carline (1889-1950) 74.7x57.8cm

What a face! I am riveted to the spot by this arresting portrait. Carline stares out of the canvas with a direct, challenging gaze. I cannot decide whether she is quizzical, aggressive, defiant or is just feeling wretched. She has dark shadows under her eyes, which she has either exaggerated or she is having an insomniac bad time. But maybe she is just looking at herself in a mirror and I have imagined everything.

Her hands are held meekly together; she is not painting. Her rather small paint box is squeezed into the lower left corner, yet being an artist was very important to her. She came from a family of artists. That cramped corner could indicate that she feels her identity as an artist is being marginalised. After all, her painter brothers rented studios opposite the family home in Hampstead, but she worked in a side passage. She and her paint box look restricted in that confining bedroom.

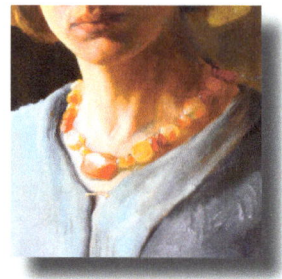

The hat might offer a clue. You do not usually wear your hat in your bedroom. It is plain and sensible and she wears it as if she is about to, or is expected to, go out and take part in social niceties; an activity that will throttle her painting time. The hat is superbly painted, with light and shade in several tones of orange. Its rim is especially exquisitely drawn, and just above her eyes on its edge is a sliver of orange that is the sort of trick that Rembrandt did with his inimitable hats. The shadow cast by the hat on her face and the light from the unseen light source are meticulously observed, as is the ribbon's end above her left shoulder.

Her necklace is quartz capsules of orange light. Her painter brothers gave it to her. It is a treasure, a beautiful feminine adornment, but she does not wear it with a flattering gown. Might she have preferred a magnificent box of paints?

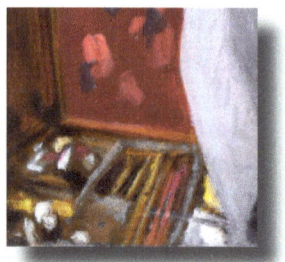

Carline is dressed for warmth, not elegance; but the large area of blue strikes a chilly note. All the other colours are in the brown/pink/orange spectrum, and this blue does not 'match'. Blue and orange complement and enhance each other, but not this blue and not this orange. Carline would know that. It is as if she is asserting her own strongly-felt identity; protesting, perhaps, at being poured into the mould of family and social expectations.

Her bedroom behind her is bold and sparely suggested in blocks of brown tones. The round object, that might be a lampshade, echoes the forms of her head and hat.

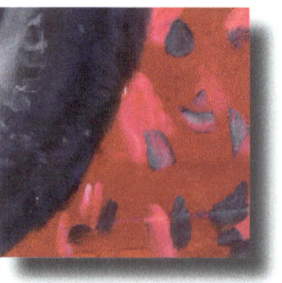

She has had great fun painting her bedspread. It is patterned with abstract splodges all over it that retain the mark of what could have been an angry brush. She liked painting it so much that it has taken on a life of its own and continues down to the bottom right edge of the picture. Everything else is painted with careful restraint, but this shows a different style, free and abandoned.

Maybe she is wondering whether she is making the right decision or a very big mistake indeed in agreeing to marry Stanley Spencer two years later.

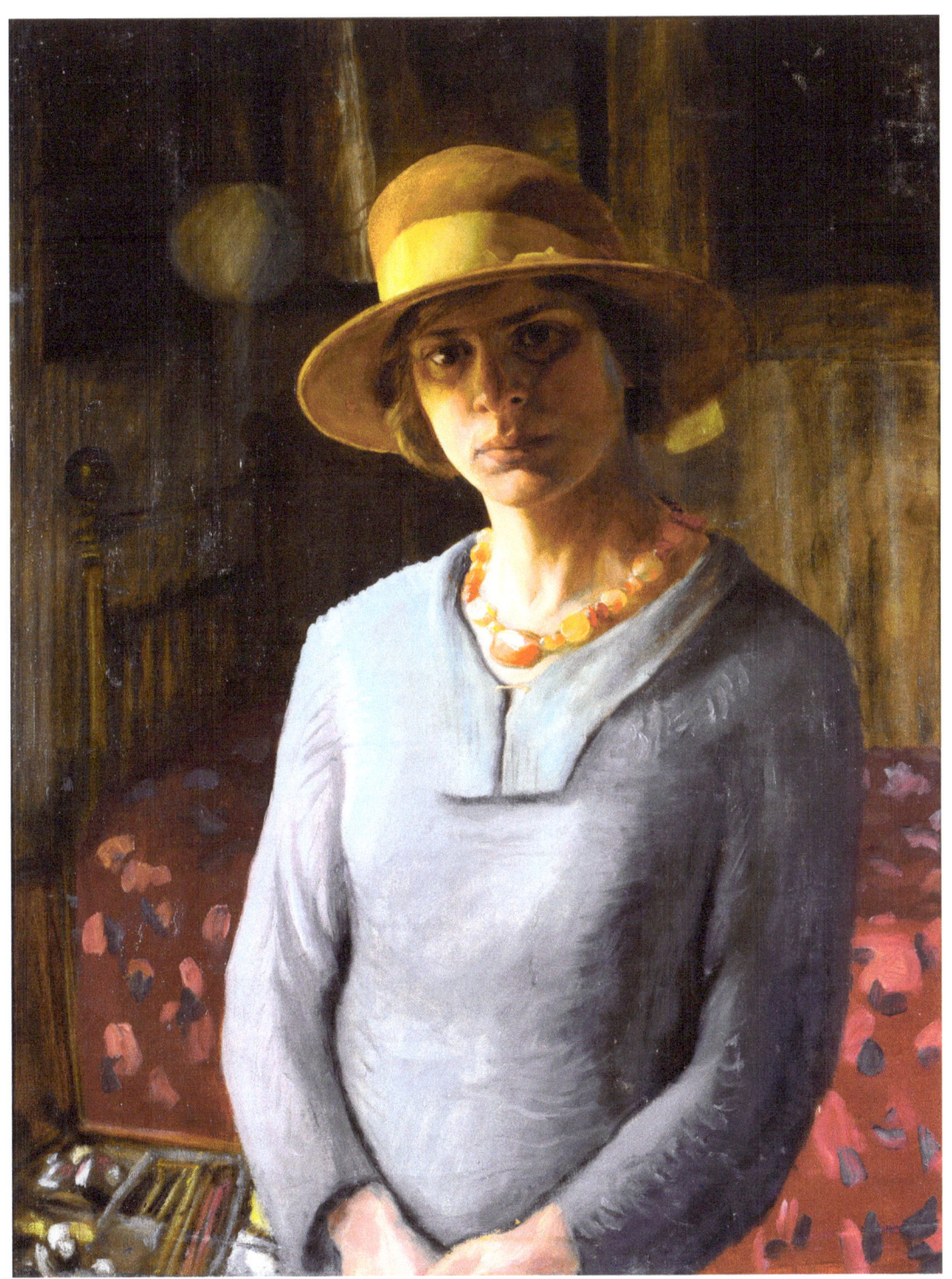

14| Toytown-by-Sea

The Hold House Port Mear Square Port Mear Beach, c1932 - Alfred Wallis (1855-1942)   30.5x38.5cm

How can we respond to the 'My child of five can do that' comment?

For this is a genuine example of naïve art, by a Cornish fisherman who never had a day's art training. Are we to take such art seriously? I will try to answer these two questions.

Wallis did not begin to paint until he was 67, after the death of his wife of 46 years. When he was 20, she had been his 43 year old widowed landlady with five children, and their own child was born three months after the marriage. Sadly, their own two children died in infancy. He had been a basket maker, a labourer and a deep sea fisherman, sailing on schooners between Penzance and Newfoundland. Later, he ran a marine store.

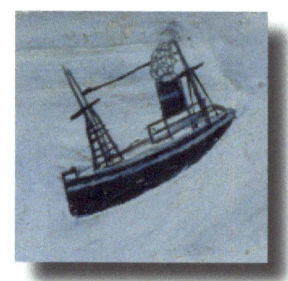

Wallis could not afford intimidating paints and canvas. He painted on anything that came to hand, such as his bellows, but mostly on odd scraps of cardboard. He bought tins of paint from a ship's chandlers; real boats could have been painted with the same paint.

His old world of sail was no more, so he painted *'what used to bee out of my memery what we may never see again'*. (His letters are in Tate's archives.)

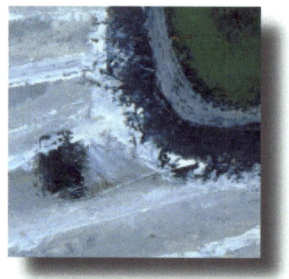

This work was painted, ironically, over an advertisement for the St Ives Society of Artists. Wallis had been taken up by St Ives artists such as Christopher Wood, Ben and Winifred Nicholson and Barbara Hepworth in 1928, otherwise we might never have heard of him. Their promotion of him, however, did not prevent his dying in the workhouse.

Wallis wrote the title of the painting on the back of it, 'hold' meaning 'old' and 'Port Mear' is 'Porthmeor.' Unmoulded by any academic discipline, perspective and scale meant nothing to him. The rocks and headland at the end of Porthmeor beach resemble an aerial map, whilst the houses are straight on. I suspect that the Old House is drawn as he saw it: there is an honesty and truth about it. The little sideways ship (he made model boats) steams towards the unseen horizon. Wallis, like Spencer in Cookham, knew every inch of what he drew. His palette, limited out of necessity, gives the picture cohesion and conviction. All is higgledy piggledy. An academic analysis of it would be foolish. He said he painted to keep himself company.

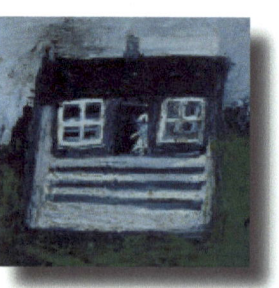

So how are we to respond to the 'child of five' comment? It is in fact a wonderful compliment and that is the whole point. Wallis has preserved the freshness of an untutored child's authentic vision, uncluttered by rules. There is an emotional involvement and intensity every bit as true as, for example, Palmer. He has painted what he feels and knows, to bring comfort to his now empty cottage. He may not have had the intellectual gifts of a 'proper' painter, but how beguiling his works are. What better reason is there to paint than to keep yourself company? Of course his utterly charming and delightful work should be taken seriously. Wallis may not have been able to spell, but he painted with compelling validity.

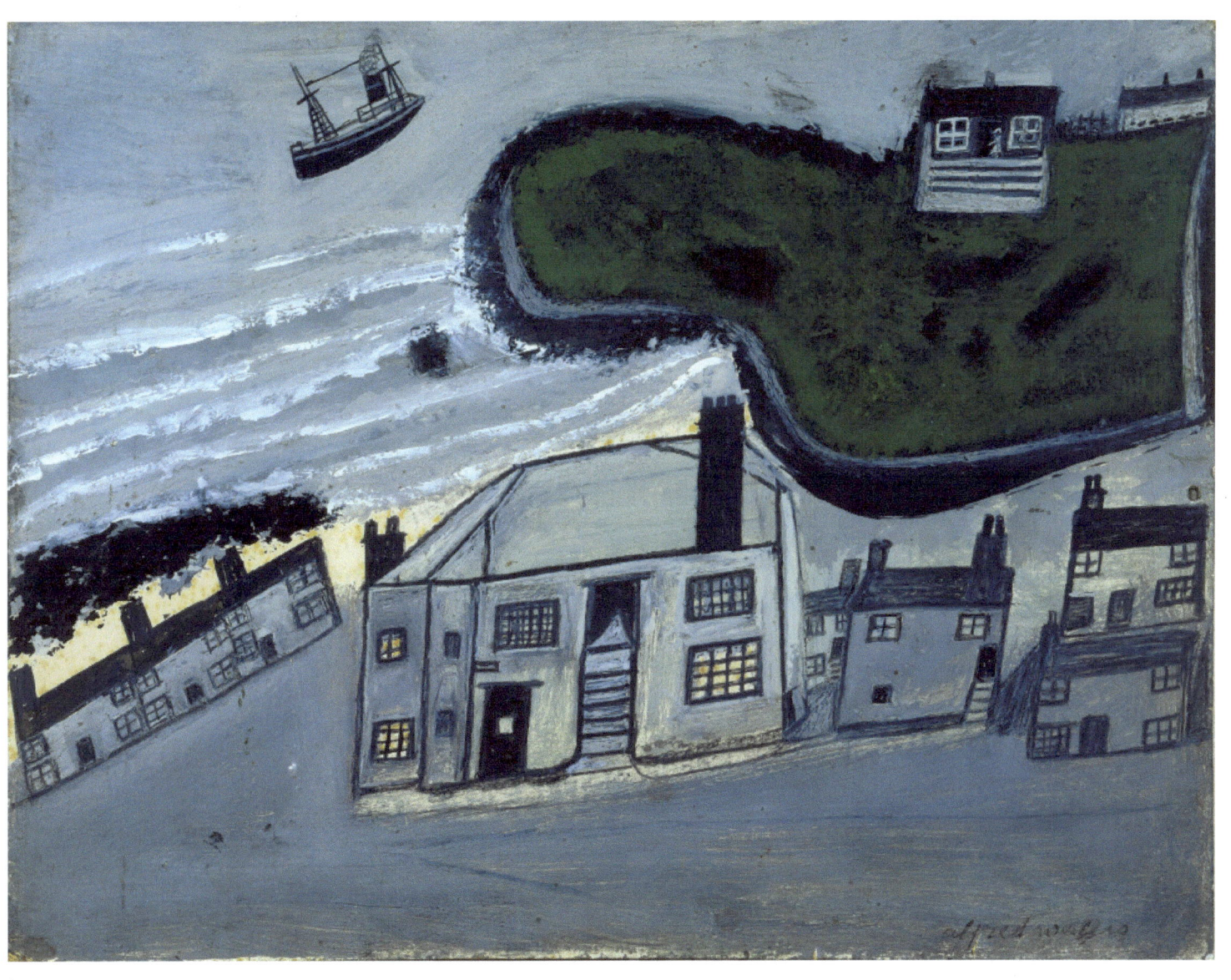

15| Battle of the Baddies

The Fall of Lucifer, 1933 - Cecil Collins MBE RA (1908-89)   273x180cm

The composition of this battle reminds me of Michelangelo's *Last Judgement* (1534-47) in the Sistine Chapel. This is not a Last Judgement, however, but possibly something even more cosmic: the expulsion of evil from good, and what happens when one loses heavenly favour.

A red Lucifer plummets head-first to earth or a steely sea, like Icarus, who has flown too close to the scarlet sun, which has melted his wings. He must have started off good to be in heaven. What did he do to deserve his fall?

Top right and left are domed shapes similar to Michelangelo's *Last Judgement*. They look like upturned vessels or heavenly jellyfish, whose tendrils appear to be angels blowing a Last Trump. This interpretation is strengthened by a naked, wingless angel who has detached himself from the group and is doing an upside-down solo.

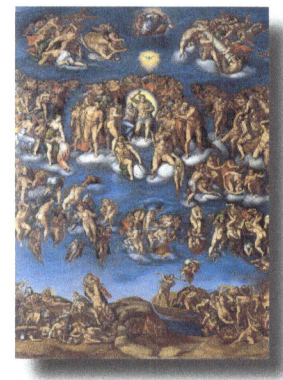

Red clouds are scattered in the yellow sky like molehills. Lucifer looks as if he will land, to be roasted alive, in a frightening brazier in the middle of the painting, where God would be if He were doing a Last Judgement. This brazier has a domed lid, and great tongues of flame are leaping from it. It could also be a squat iron devil with a metal hat, its mouth full of fire and its teeth gnashing. If this monstrous furnace does not get Lucifer, there are six jagged rocks rising from a striated sea or land to pierce him.

On either side, large protective angels with blue wings shelter and guard groups of naked figures, who have curious, almost el Greco, proportions. They have no gender identification, so they could be the saved goodies, but there are only eleven of them. They watch, leaning precariously from a cliff-top on the left and a large boulder on the right. They seem unable to intervene.

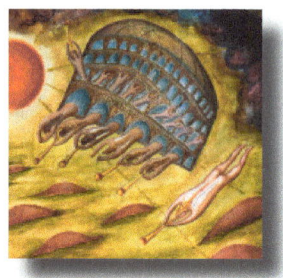

On the edge of the left hand cliff is a small grey animal. I would like to think that it is the Lamb of God, but it is unlikely. A figure in the middle of the right hand group is clothed in filmy white: perhaps s/he is a newly-dead soul who has been given the robe of righteousness.

The result of Lucifer's expulsion from heaven is a great battle in the lower foreground, with naked and clothed figures, some with wings. Possibly the clothed figures are earthly baddies and the naked are heavenly goodies, but all wield swords and shields, fighting and killing. Did they arm themselves from heaven's store or find weapons on earth? One winged figure on the right swoops down, sword in hand. The good have stopped being good.

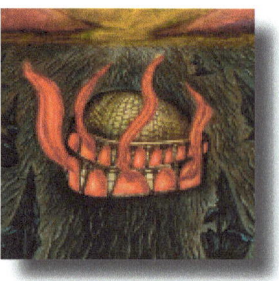

Heaven is above, hell is in the middle and hell on earth is at the bottom. Good cannot help or stop evil and, moreover, participates in it. It is a dark message if I am right.

Who is missing? Surely it is God, who has seen what man has done with His creation. He has expelled Lucifer, appointed angels to guard the few whom He has saved, and has left the scene in disgust.

Who can blame Him?

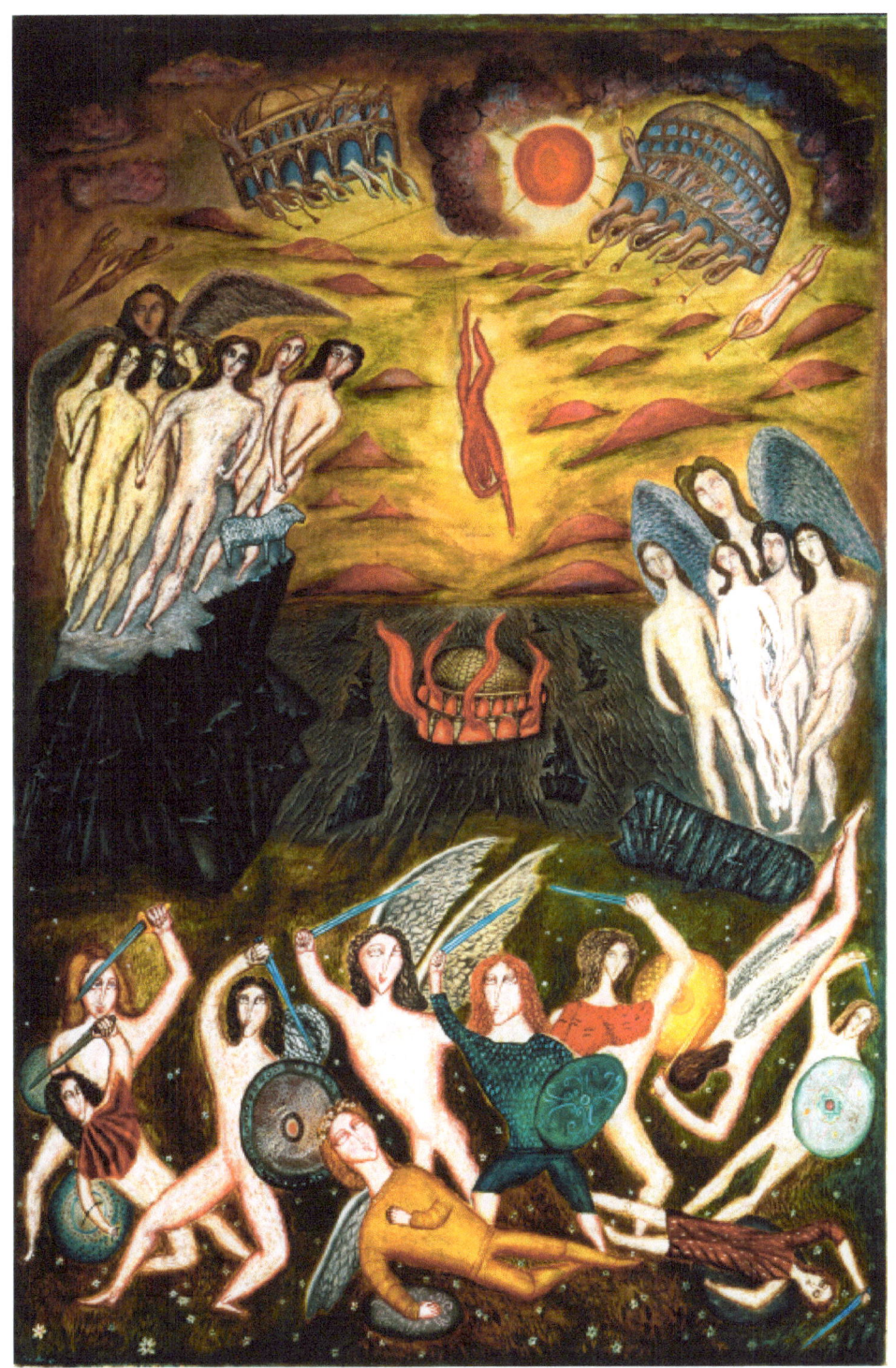

16| Triptych of Terror
Three Studies for Figures at the Base of a Crucifixion, c1944 - Francis Bacon (1910-92)   each panel 94.0x73.7cm

"I wouldn't want that on my wall" is the old chestnut comment. Indeed nor would I, but I find it compelling nonetheless.

It is painted on three separate panels, hung together as a triptych, as if it were a fifteenth century Virgin and Saints; but the content is as far from that subject matter as is possible.

Ever since David Sylvester's conversations with Bacon were published,* we know what was in Bacon's mind in 1944. We know his references to the Eumenides or Erinyes, who were Greek furies, the Greek gods' instruments of vengeance. We read of the trilogy of savage and broody dramas the Oresteia of Aeschylus. There are obvious references to Picasso and Eisenstein's Russian Revolution film *The Battleship Potemkin* in 1925, with the close-up of the woman who had been shot in the face. We hear that Bacon was drawn to depictions of screaming mouths and diseases of the mouth, and how suffering and terror are expressed in the face.

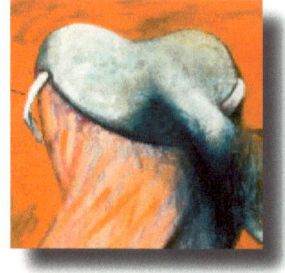

Reading the conversations, however, comes between me and looking hard and long at these panels. The two left-hand ones are smeared with a darker orange than the right hand one. Orange should be a cheerful colour, but this shade is disturbing. The vague perspective lines indicate claustrophobia and confinement, or the pointlessness of depicting space.

The form on the left is bowed in agony towards the central panel. Although its long neck stretches from the shape of a valentine heart, that heart is dead and grey. Love is absent. Its extremity of suffering is expressed by its having no limbs but flipper 'arms.' It cannot move, it has been put on some sort of chair and is collapsing in anguish.

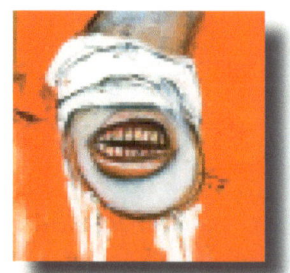

The middle amorphous blob has a small platform on legs in front of it. It is blindfolded, and screams into an orange abyss of terror, horror, pain or whatever afflicts it. If the orange is blood, even that colour has been distorted.

The right-hand shape extends its neck towards the centre panel. It stands on a mat of nails. It has no need of a blindfold as it has no eyes, only an ear and a mouth that lets out a primeval scream.

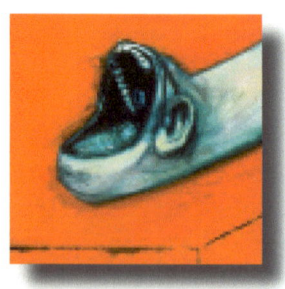

The whole triptych is profoundly distressing. No wonder it caused a furore when it was exhibited in 1945. That date must surely be pivotal. The war had caused untold suffering. The triptych could also be the forms that were once people in the Holocaust ovens. No image is horrific enough to express that.

Surely art is not just to soothe and confirm us in what we already know, what is safe and cosy. If art is to reflect reality and truth, it should not flinch from truth that we cannot bear.

If we have experienced the human condition we may even find these images ultimately cathartic.

*Sylvester D, *Conversations with Francis Bacon* (London and New York, Thames and Hudson, 1994)

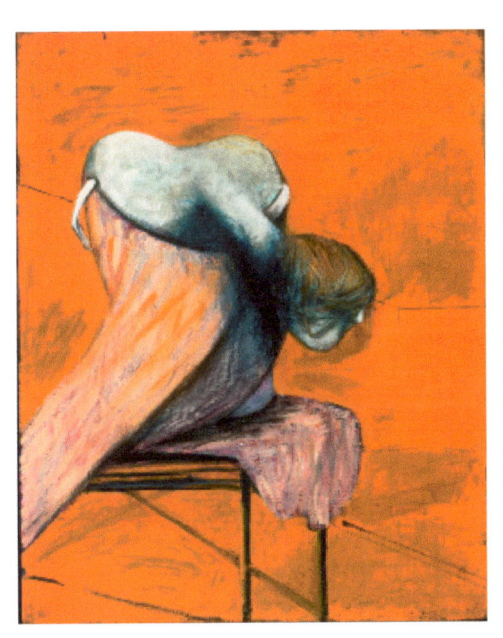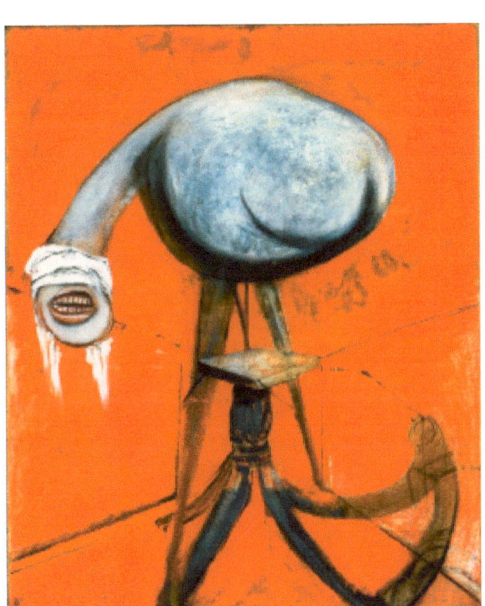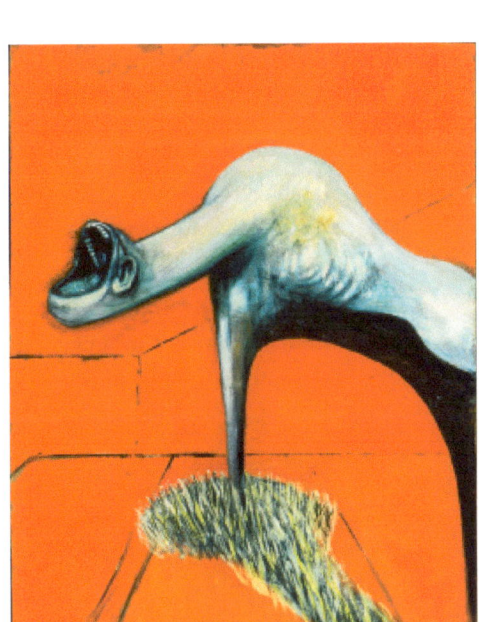

17| Notes for Goats
Pastoral for PW, 1948 - John Craxton (1922-2009) 197x259cm

What I think is so clever about this painting is that it is chock-full of influences from past art, and yet Craxton has created an authentic vision that is entirely his own. Only great artists like Picasso can absorb other paintings whole, and invent, not a pastiche, but highly original work that pushes artistic boundaries into untrodden realms. This is what I think Craxton has done.

It is a joyous celebration of life in a pastoral landscape, painted for Craxton's friend Peter Watson, who collected modern paintings, supported the arts and paid for Craxton's studio, which he shared for a while with Lucien Freud. It was in Watson's home in London that Craxton first saw works by Picasso and Sutherland; he later painted with Sutherland in Pembrokeshire in 1943-4, and met Picasso in 1946.

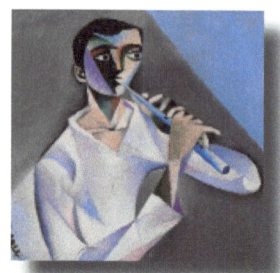

Fresh from these meetings, one can see the influences on him of Picasso in the pink goat on the right, especially its neck; and Sutherland around the off-centre tree. As if Picasso and Sutherland were not enough inspiration for Craxton, Watson also first showed him reproductions of work by Samuel Palmer, whose essence Craxton has distilled here. He owes an acknowledged debt to the pastoral landscapes of Blake and Palmer, but Palmer's cosy hills are rounded, and these are pointed pyramids of rapture.

So Peter Watson certainly deserves the dedication of this painting to him.

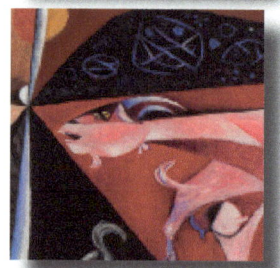

One can see elements here of Cubism, perhaps Futurism and Chagall; but Cubism, at least that by Picasso and Braque, was monochromatic. This is a jubilant revelry in colour, and more particularly of music and Greece. Craxton came from a large musical family, and he also first visited Greece in 1946 because he heard it was like Pembrokeshire, eventually spending 50 of his 87 years there.

It is almost as if this landscape is doing a biblical 'clapping its hands in joy.' The goats, which may or may not be capricious portraits of Craxton's friends, frolic jerkily in their prismatic patchwork peaks. Craxton said that the flautist was 'an emblematic me,' but he is also the Greeks Orpheus, Dionysius and Pan: music, fruitfulness and fertility. His white clothes speak of a primal innocence.

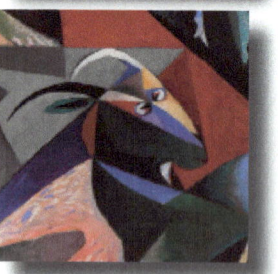

Craxton's own words could not express it better:

"I wanted to safeguard a private world of mystery and I was drawn to the idea of bucolic calm as a kind of refuge."

This is very Palmer.

So 'Pastoral for PW' is the complete expression of the lyrical world that Craxton wanted to 'safeguard'. His recipe for it is: equal amounts of Blake, Palmer, Picasso, Sutherland and Chagall; but, most of all, a bag full of the sifted flour of his own intensely original creative power.

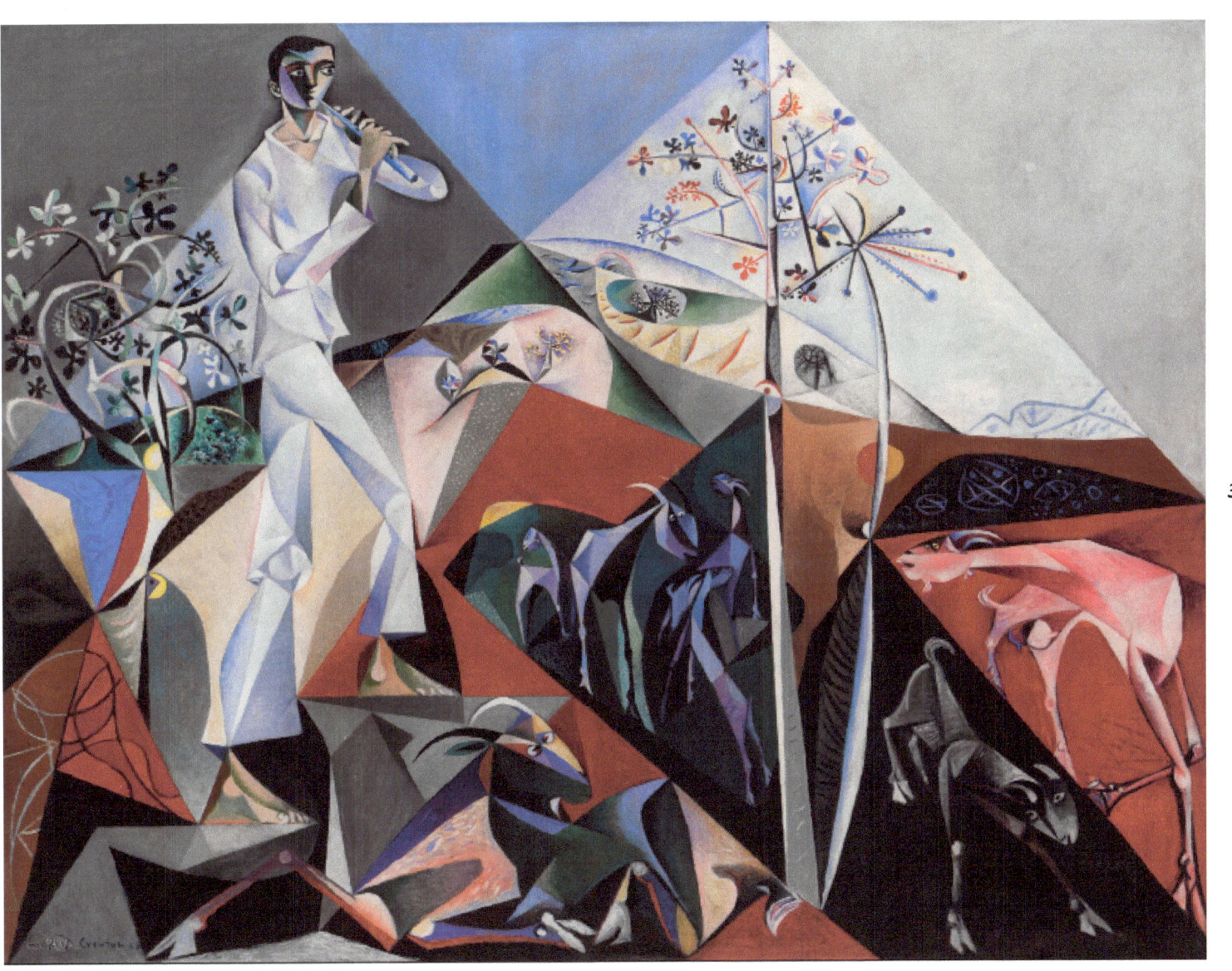

18| The Power of Paint

Lost Mine, 1959 - Peter Lanyon (1918 - 1964)   183.2x152.7cm

I am sorry that Lanyon gave this title to his painting, because then I start to look for a lost mine. To me, the canvas is about paint. Without reading the explanatory label, I sense violence and destruction; but I also see the wild movement of Lanyon's arm as he hurtles paint on to the canvas. If I turn a postcard reproduction of it upside-down and sideways, I feel the same intensity.

Turning to the wall label, I learn that the artist is not depicting a scene, but the experience of being at a place. He is also evoking its historical past. The painting, I read, was inspired by Levant in Cornwall, where many men were drowned when the sea inundated the tin mines that had been tunnelled under it.

However abstract a painting is, viewers will make associations, so sense and order can be imposed. The descriptive title Lost Mine encourages this, unfortunately.

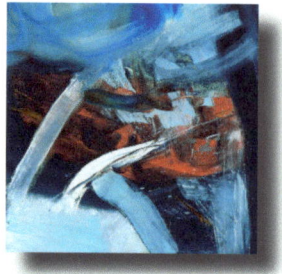

Having read that, I feel directed to see mine walls, firm on the left and buckling on the right, as the sea roars and plunges through, drowning all in its path. Red is inevitably linked to blood. The swirling coils at the top right could evoke miners trying to rise above the flood. Black could be terror and destruction, and the black scribbles on the right could suggest miners desperately clawing at the breaking walls.

I mentally tuck the label behind the frame and look again, as I do not want to make associations. The canvas does not tell a story in the conventional sense, and has freed the great slashes of paint to be just that – paint on canvas. It need stand for nothing but itself in all its forceful energy. There is an immediacy of mark-making and an urgency of communication.

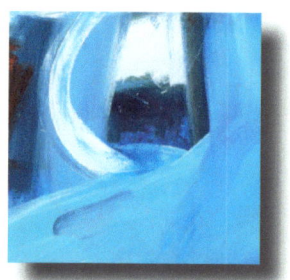

It may look like an unconsidered abstract muddle, but every wide- brushed splurge of paint plays its part in the overall design. The bent black vertical, the scribble on its right, each arc, each block of colour, is exactly where it should be. Move them about and the picture does not work. In particular, the red area is a lynchpin; cover it up on a postcard reproduction and the painting is robbed of a vital life force. Take out the white and the canvas is dull. Every mark matters.

The remarkable thing is that the painting communicates emotion through its very abstraction, without the title. Each viewer will feel something different, for the value of non-figurative painting is that, freed of only one possible interpretation, there is a multiplicity of significance and meaning. To cite examples: Stubbs has painted horses, Fildes a sick child, and Nicholson a bowl. That is what the paintings are about. Here it is what the paint is doing that communicates.

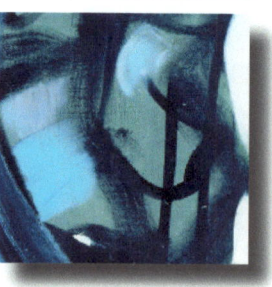

I feel with terrific force the violent breaking through and forward momentum of the blue towards me. The broken marks all around that blue have an expressive urgency of panic and fear. To depict this in a narrative way might have lessened the extreme emotion.

By harnessing the ability of paint marks alone to communicate, Lanyon has affected me profoundly.

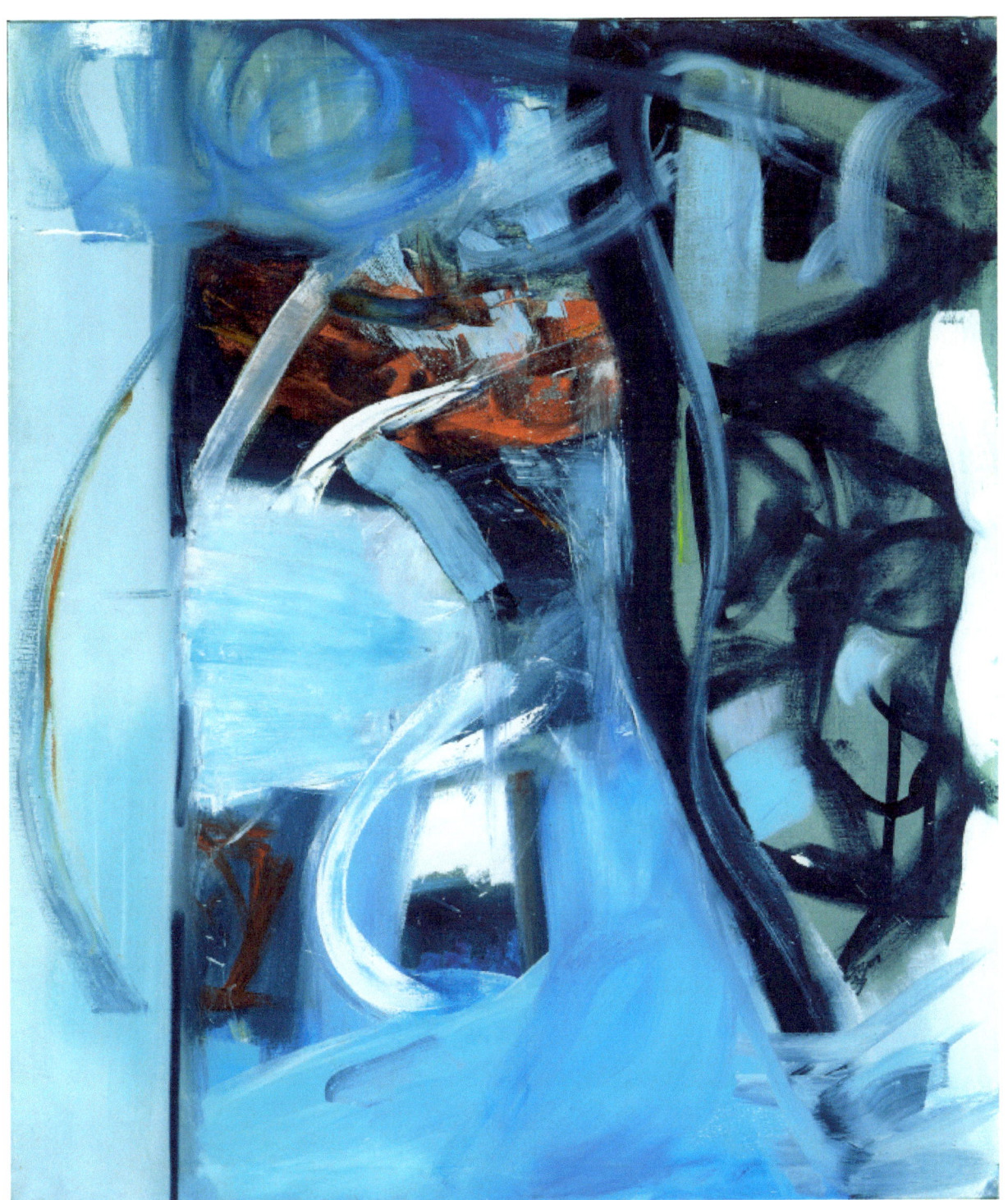

19| Interior with Shapes

Mr and Mrs Clark and Percy, 1970-71 - David Hockney (1937-)   213.4x304.8cm

This interior mesmerises me. I am held in thrall by its silence, balance and order, and yet there is a tension amongst the calm arrangements. I think this is achieved by strong abstract elements that still retain the realism of observed life and the photographs that Hockney worked from.

What I mean by 'abstract elements' are compositional lines and the reduction of objects to inter-related shapes that have an identity beyond that which they represent; somehow managing to give meaning and atmosphere.

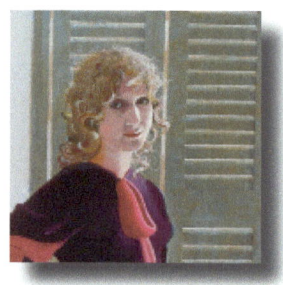

In 1969 Hockney had been best man at the wedding of his friends Ossie Clark and Celia Birtwell, fashion and fabric designers respectively. Here, Ossie sits, Celia stands; she is a powerful pink and purple vertical. Apart from her, the colours harmonise, but she does not belong to the colour scheme, or possibly not in the marriage; but one does not want information to detract from looking at structure and pattern. In fact, the purple of her robe is picked up in Ossie's left foot, the 'leaves' of the lamp and the shadow behind it. The hem of her gown touches and follows the line of the table, her arm making a triangle like that of Ossie's chair back. There is a small smile on her delicate face, with the light half on it, but no smile in her eyes. The painting would lack dynamism if she, too, were in blue and green; nevertheless her dark colours jar and give her a disturbing presence, making me tense.

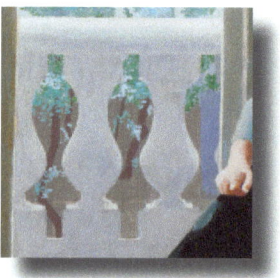

Ossie's body language slants away from his wife, possibly indicative of their eventual divorce. He slumps and sulks in a style-statement chair, making a dramatic diagonal which the table continues, but which his forward-angled head counteracts. Ossie belongs here, his clothes match the colours inside and out. He ignores the cat, whose fur links with other white areas. The tactile rug, its pile as pale and curly as Celia's hair, looks softly warm, but the rest feels emotionally chilly. The design and colours alone have conveyed a mood of uneasiness.

Other ordered shapes calm me, however. The table on the left makes an oblique angle, with two other subtly different slanting angles on it: the book and the shadow of the vase. The picture on the wall above, which is one of Hockney's etchings, is a face-on rectangle, and two related oblongs are the windows of the house opposite. The white and turquoise of the sparely painted lilies and their slender vase are balanced by the lamp and telephone behind Ossie.

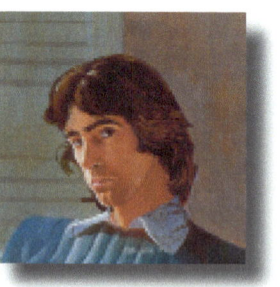

Strong verticals are made by the windows and shutters with horizontal slats of light coming through the left shutter and darker slats on the right. Outside tones echo those inside, uniting them. I am calmer still.

The balcony balustrade is clever and witty: one sees simultaneously the white positive shape of the vertical struts and the background negative shapes of foliage and twigs. The eye alternates between them in a visual game.

I find this painting entirely satisfying intellectually: it is like a structured, well-designed meccano set that is somehow able to convey mood and meaning in one magnificent whole. Hockney's art has many pinnacles: this is one.

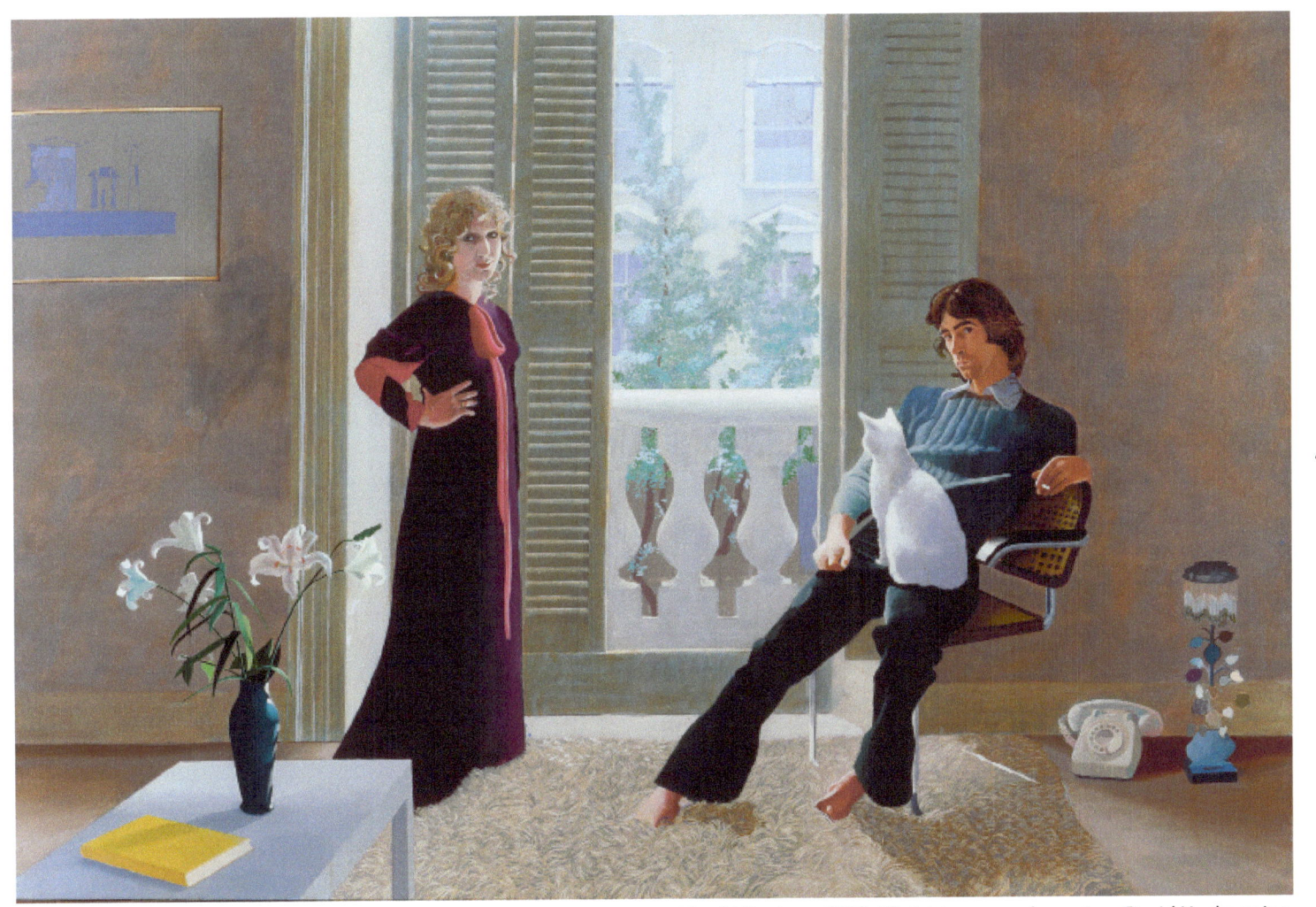

20| Kaleidoscope

Nataraja, 1993 - Bridget Riley (1931-)   165.1x227.7cm

Standing before this heart-lifting map of colour is an overwhelmingly exultant experience. It is a wildly exciting and joyful painting.

Nataraja means Lord of the Dance, from Hindu mythology. He is the Hindu god Shiva in his form as the cosmic dancer, usually shown with several arms.

It is like looking at a sunlit scene, the eye travelling over it without a focal point, with vertical bands and repeating diagonals of colour. One certainly feels the rhythm and jerky movement of a dance implied by the title.

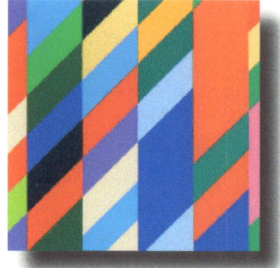

Riley may not have done the actual application of the paint on this canvas herself, as from the 1960s she has employed assistants. However, it is a highly organised painting, every inch of which she has worked out and controlled.

Each colour also has an exact size that gives it its full intensity. Some are opaque, some seemingly transparent. As you watch, some colours appear to recede and others advance. Dark shades should recede and light ones advance, but sometimes it is the other way round and at other times they do both simultaneously. It is an entrancing pattern of the full spectrum in a prismatic dazzling of the eye.

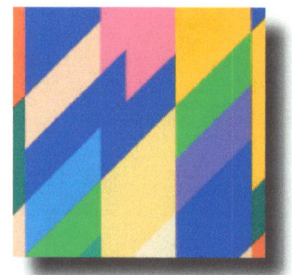

Nataraja is a highly technical exploration of what colour can do by itself. It is not limited by a description of any recognisable form, which would tie it down to representation and interpretation, but is a panoply of glorious hues. The juxtapositions are dizzyingly clever. Each colour is placed next to its neighbour with reverential care so that its unmodulated purity is enhanced. Riley knows exactly what she is doing and is leaving nothing to chance.

For example, orange next to pink can look a different tone from when it is placed next to the shade of blue that is its complementary. The brightest of the zinging greens appears to change when adjacent to red. A pink parallelogram needs to be a certain size to give it its full strength and effect. Pale yellow is needed here, and a deeper yellow there. The white bands are crucial, making the colour next to them appear to be even more intense. There is no black to make holes or cause a negative emotion. No block could be taken away, made a different size, replaced, or put next to a different colour without disturbing the pattern's poise.

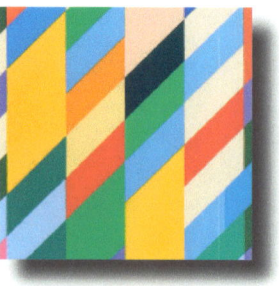

Sights, sounds and tastes often evoke memories; and if they are happy memories, one likes the cause of it. For me I am a child again endlessly gazing into my kaleidoscope, turning the end of it so that the little lozenges of scattered colour assemble and reassemble into different patterns. I thought it was utterly magical. I sat up a tree, out of the way of jobs, spellbound. This is probably why I so love this explosion of colour that looks at first sight to be random.

Just as a figurative painting can yield layer after layer of meaning to me, so can gazing at *Nataraja* nourish my very soul with its kaleidoscope of colour.

What more can I ask of a painting than that it makes me feel happy?

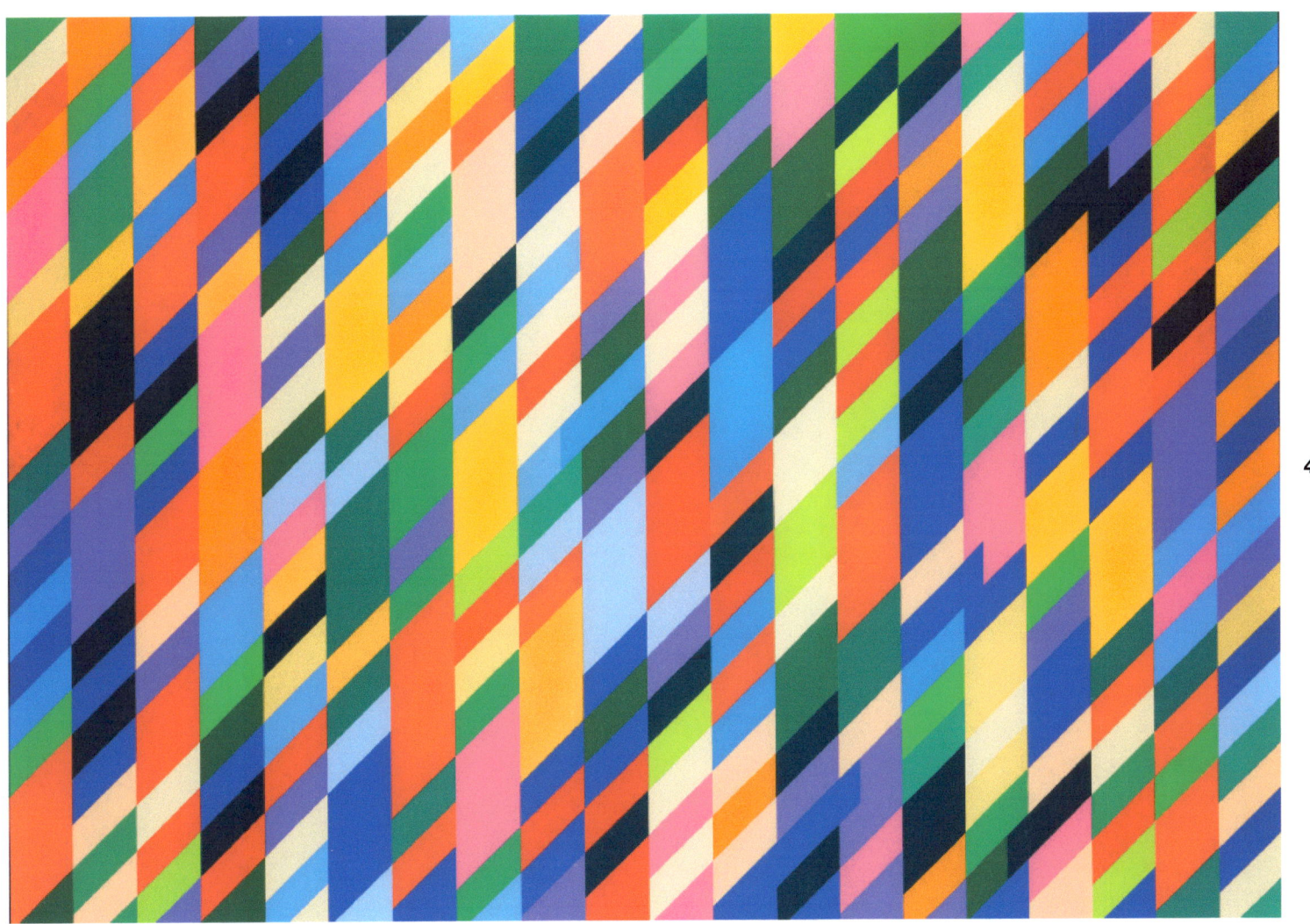

©Bridget Riley 2012. All rights reserved, courtesy Karsten Schubert, London

www.ingramcontent.com/pod-product-compliance
Lightning Source LLC
Chambersburg PA
CBHW040410220526
45473CB00004B/1193